Word History:

A Guide to Understanding the English Language

by

Carl B. Smith

and

Eugene W. Reade

ERIC Clearinghouse on Reading and Communication Skills

Published by:

ERIC Clearinghouse on Reading and Communication Skills
Carl B. Smith, Director
Smith Research Center Suite 150
2805 East 10th Street
Indiana University
Bloomington, Indiana 47408-2698

1991

Typesetting and design at ERIC/RCS and printing by Indiana University Printing Services.

This publication was prepared with funding from the Office of Educational Research and Improvement, U.S. Department of Education, under contract no. RI88062001. Contractors undertaking such projects under government sponsorship are encouraged to express freely their judgment in professional and technical matters. Points of view or opinions, however, do not necessarily represent the official view or opinions of the Office of Educational Research and Improvement.

Library of Congress Cataloging-in-Publication Data

Smith, Carl Bernard.
   Word history : a guide to understanding the English language / by Carl B. Smith and Eugene W. Reade.

   p. cm.

   Includes biographical references.

   ISBN 0-927516-12-8

   1. English language—History Outlines, syllabi, etc. 2. English language—Word formation. 3. English language—Etymology.
   I. Smith, Carl B., 1932-   . II. Reade, Eugene W., 1935-   . III. Title.
   PE1093.S6 1989   89-25837
   420.9—dc20   CIP

Acknowledgements

The diagram on Indo-European languages on page 3 is adapted from *The Random House Dictionary of the English Language,* Second Edition, Unabridged (Random House, 1987), front endpaper, and is reprinted by permission.

The page from Benjamin Franklin's book *Idea of the English School*, reproduced on page 74, is taken from C. William Miller, *Benjamin Franklin's Philadelphia Printing* (American Philosophical Society, 1974), p. 283, and is reprinted by permission.

Table of Contents

Introduction

Our English vocabulary is not something to be studied in
isolation but is related in one way or another to many of the
other languages of the world. The proper beginning for us,
therefore, is to view the place of English in perspective, amid
the many tongues of mankind. (Ayers, 1986, p. 1)

Language-arts teachers in the upper grades can see the
relevance of this statement as they work with their students in
the classroom. At a conference of educators held in Indianapolis
in the summer of 1989, a junior-high-school teacher bragged
about the effect that the study of Latin and Greek words was
having on vocabulary development in her classes. Even more
exciting, she said, was her students' increased interest in words
and how they developed. She was sure that her students were
deriving great benefits from their study of word roots and origins.

This teacher helped her students discover that studying the
history of the English language can lead to a clearer understanding of why we write and speak as we do today. Your students will find that this study will help them in a number of
ways. They will see growth in **vocabulary** as they become
aware of how words have been absorbed from other languages
and sometimes altered to conform to conventions of the English
language. This study will help with **spelling** by contributing to
a better understanding of the structure of words that follow
fairly regular patterns, especially those derived from Latin.
Students will come to realize that other words which may seem
odd at first glance have in fact evolved from patterns that were
logical and regular at some time in the past. They will also gain
a greater appreciation of earlier literature as they become
aware of the importance of **semantics**—a knowledge of the
meanings of words and how those meanings may change with
time. Finally, students will become aware of the importance of
etymology—the study of the history of words as they developed
from their early forms in ancient languages.

Our purpose is to help teachers in the upper grades lead their students toward an understanding of the history of English. This guide presents a brief survey of the history of the language, focusing on outside influences as well as on characteristics of the language and its literature. At the end of each chapter we have provided a few exercises suggesting ways in which students may work with the language of that period. These exercises will help make historical knowledge a meaningful part of the study of English.

If you have not already studied language history, then this survey will give you a starting point. If you have studied this history, then the survey can offer a review while providing the core of information to present to students.

We hope that this guide will demonstrate the value of studying language history and will provide material and suggestions you can use to complement your language-arts program. Its goal is to make your students aware of the development of the English language and to help them understand more fully the reasons for current conventions of spelling and grammar. "To understand how things are, it is often helpful and sometimes essential to know how they got to be that way" (Pyles and Algeo, 1982, p. 2).

See the companion volume, **Word History: A Resource Book for the Teacher**, published by ERIC/RCS. A further collection of language exercises, information, and pointers for using sources in the ERIC database, this complementary volume will enable you to incorporate historical study into your language-arts program.

Chapter I

The Origin of English

Similarities among Languages

If we compare the English words *mother* and *father* with their counterparts in a number of other languages, we discover that they have much in common:

German	Dutch	Danish	Latin	Greek	Persian
Mutter	moeder	moder	māter	mētēr	mādar
Vater	vader	fader	pater	patēr	pidar

These are only a few of the many examples that can be cited to show that English is related to several other languages.

Ever since the twelfth century, scholars have been aware that some European languages shared a number of common features. It was not until 1786, however, that anyone attempted a comprehensive explanation for these similarities. In that year Sir William Jones, a British government official who had served in India, set forth a hypothesis based on his study of Sanskrit. Jones insisted that the Sanskrit, Latin, Greek, Germanic, and Celtic languages were not only related but were in fact descended from a single source (Millward, 1989, pp. 43-44). This ancient source language, called *Proto-Indo-European* (PIE), is often identified simply as *Indo-European* (IE). Although there is no written record of the IE language, scholars have been able to reconstruct it to a certain extent by comparing the similar features of those related languages that do have a written record.

Indo-European Languages

The common language and culture of the Indo-European people flourished in central Europe approximately 7,000 to 8,000 years ago. Although opinions differ, it is likely that the homeland of the Indo-Europeans was the area to the north or west of the Black Sea, perhaps near the valley of the Danube River (Claiborne, 1983, pp. 36-43). This culture gradually disintegrated as some tribes left central Europe and moved westward as far as Britain and Iceland; others moved toward Persia and India in the east. As these tribes became more and more isolated from their homeland and from each other, their speech began to evolve into the various languages shown in the diagram on page three.

Two branches of the *Germanic* language are of greatest concern to us. One of these, *West Germanic,* was brought to Britain in the fifth century by people who originally lived along the North Sea coast of Europe: it is the parent tongue of the English we speak today. A related form, *North Germanic,* was spoken by the Scandinavians who began to invade and occupy portions of Britain beginning in the late eighth century.

The other branches of greatest importance to the development of English are the *Italic,* especially Latin and French, and the *Hellenic,* the language of ancient Greece. Another branch, the *Celtic,* included the speech of those Indo-European people who had migrated to Britain from the continent as early as the seventh century B.C. The culture and language of the Celts, overwhelmed and shunted aside by later invasions from the continent, did not play a major role in the development of English itself.

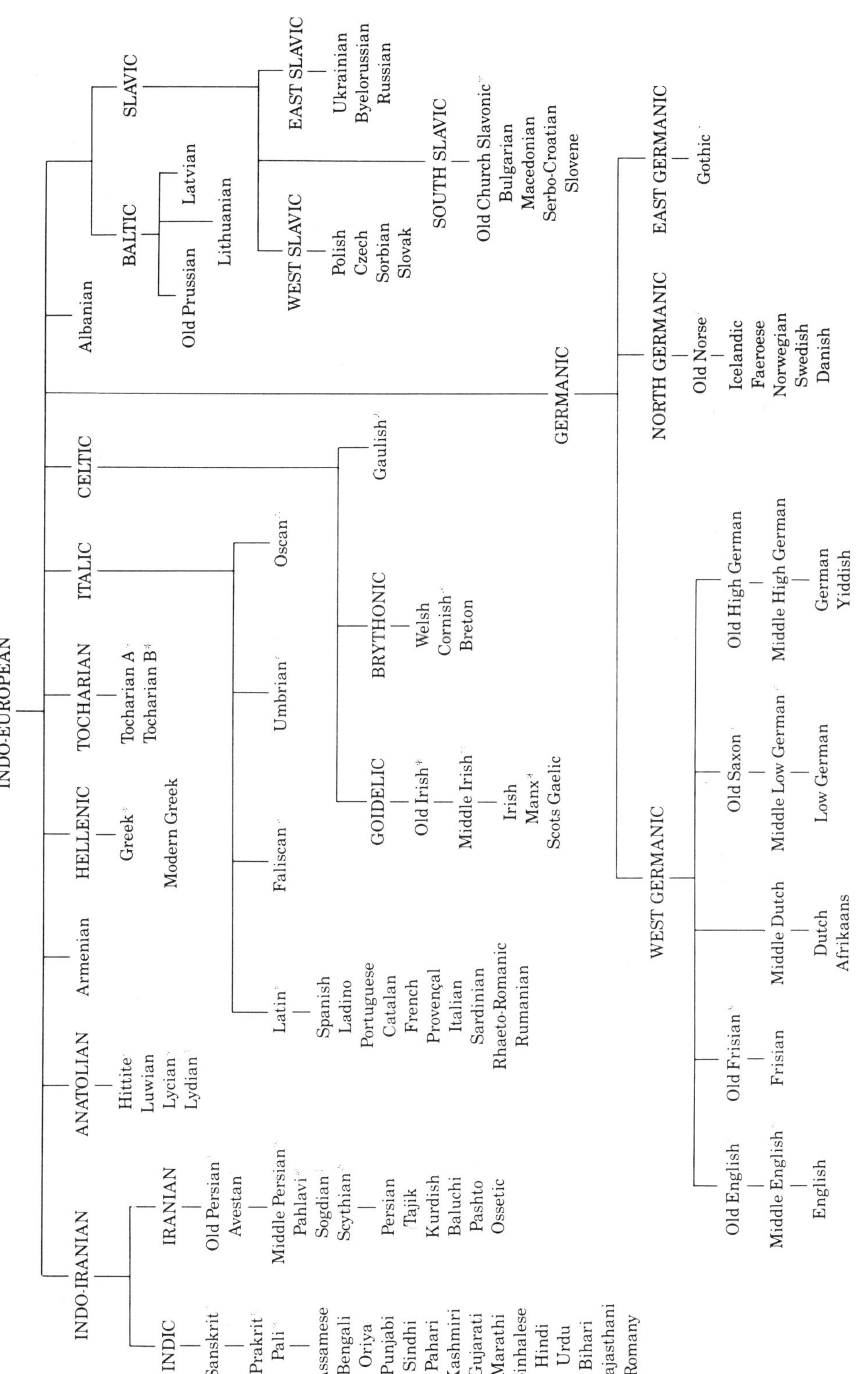

Indo-European Languages

(Adapted from *The Random House Dictionary of the English Language* [1987], front endpaper.)

Periods in the History of English

Even though English began as one of the Germanic languages, it changed dramatically as it was influenced by other languages brought into Britain over the centuries. We can better understand how English developed if we first look at the time line below, showing the important dates and prominent features of each period.

Old English 450 - 1100	Middle English 1100 - 1500	Modern English 1500 - present
West Germanic in vocabulary	French and more Latin words added	Vocabulary enriched by Greek and still more Latin words
Fully inflected	Inflections simplified	
Stress on root syllable	Some older Germanic words eliminated	Some earlier spellings remain; pronunciations change (Great Vowel Shift)
Strong and weak verb conjugations		
	Standard literary English emerges	
Oral tradition in epic poetry		Standard spellings are gradually established
Latin influence from 597 on	Printing makes books available (1476)	

Periods in the History of English

Old English
(c. 450 – 1100)

External History

The Celts: Early Inhabitants of Britain

About 2,500 years ago Britain was inhabited by tribes of Celtic people who had migrated from central Europe. These people called their new home the *Pretannic Islands* and called themselves *Pretanni*. Dialects of their language are still spoken in some areas of Wales, Ireland, Scotland, and in the French coastal region of Brittany.

In 55 B.C. Julius Caesar undertook his first expedition to the island he called *Britannia*, where he encountered the Celtic people called the *Britons*. Caesar did not remain in *Britannia* for very long, but in A.D. 43 the Roman Emperor Claudius began a determined campaign to conquer Britain and bring it into his empire. For some 350 years the island was occupied by Roman forces who controlled much of the area now known as England. The *Latin* language of these Roman armies can still be seen in inscriptions on stone monuments in England today.

The Roman and Celtic civilizations coexisted as long as Roman legions remained in Britain, and the Celtic people continued to speak their own language while borrowing a number of words from Latin. The Latin language did eventually play a most important role in the development of English, but its major influence began almost two hundred years after Roman armies had left Britain.

Germanic Tribes: Invasion from Northern Europe

By A.D. 410 the Roman legions had returned to Italy to protect their native land from attacks by migrating peoples from northern Europe. Germanic tribes living along the North Sea coast ventured into Britain in the fourth and fifth centuries; by 449 these tribes began to occupy the island in earnest. The speech of these newcomers established the foundation for English, and their Germanic tongue continued to provide a framework as English changed under the influence of other languages in later centuries.

The most important Germanic peoples to occupy Britain were the Angles, Saxons, Jutes, and Frisians. These tribes originally lived in the areas now called Denmark, northern Germany, and the Netherlands. The map on page 7 shows the movement of these tribes into areas along the eastern and southern coasts of the British Isles. Today we often refer to these tribes collectively as the *Anglo-Saxons*; the Celts called them all *Saxons*, regardless of their origin. The Germanic name of the Angles was *Angli*, which they changed to *Engle* after arriving in Britain. The *Engle* eventually called their country *Englaland*, "land of the Engle," and later this name became *England.*

Roman Missionaries: Return of the Latin Language to Britain

The language of the Anglo-Saxons began to establish the basis for English during the period from the middle of the fifth century until the end of the sixth century. Then in 597 the *Latin* language was brought back into England by missionaries traveling from Rome. Unlike the earlier period when Britain was occupied by Roman armies, the Latin language now played an important role in the development of English. These missionaries not only introduced Latin words into the English language but also employed an alphabet that was well adapted to recording literary works. Latin interacted with Anglo-Saxon to establish not only the **lexicon**—the complete store of base words, inflections, and affixes—but also the grammatical structure that enabled English to absorb the influence of other languages in centuries to come.

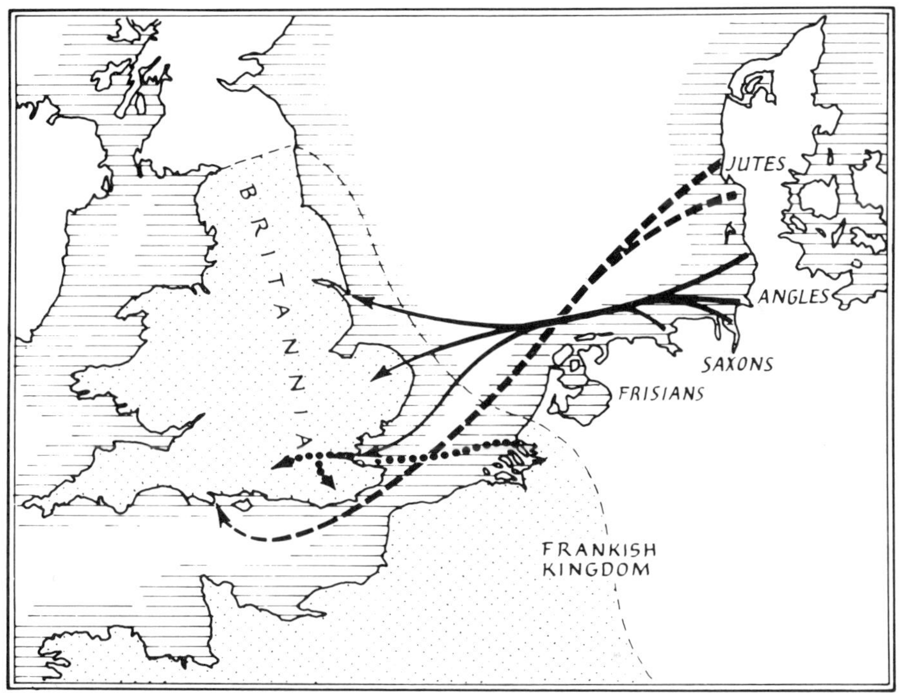

Movement of Germanic Tribes into Britain (Collins, 1988, p. 13)

During the seventh and eighth centuries, England became a center of learning as church schools were established and scholars taught the language and literature of Greece and Rome as well as the other disciplines that formed the basis of medieval learning. In fact, "the level of Latin scholarship was so high in England that English scholars were in demand on the Continent. Alcuin of York became director of Charlemagne's Palace School" (Millward, 1989, p. 68). This body of classical learning had a great impact on Old English language and verse. More and more Latin words were added to the store of Germanic words, and the oral tradition of Anglo-Saxon verse began to be recorded by Latin scribes who were the first to use English as a *written* language.

Viking Raiders: The Influence of the Danes

Beginning in the late eighth century, Britain was invaded and occupied once again—this time, by Vikings from Norway and Denmark. The Vikings were also called *Norsemen* (Northmen), but the Anglo-Saxons usually referred to them collectively as the *Danes*. These Scandinavian tribes should not be confused with the Anglo-Saxons themselves, who had come to Britain from areas of Denmark and northern Germany three or four hundred years earlier. In fact, the Vikings considered the Anglo-Saxon English as enemies to be conquered, and England as a land to be occupied.

Historical records of the period tell of the terror felt by the English when Viking raiders first attacked the eastern coast of England in 787. The Danes continued their attacks and occupied more and more of the country until they were stopped in 878 by King Alfred the Great. Many monasteries were destroyed during this century of Viking raids, leaving few scholars or seats of learning in England.

The Danes later broke the truce of 878, but King Alfred defeated them once again and succeeded in conquering London in 886. An uneasy coexistence between the Danes and the English lasted until the eleventh century, when more Viking raiders from Scandinavia descended on Britain. One major effect of this Danish occupation was the expansion of the Anglo-Saxon lexicon as additional words from Old Norse, the language of these Scandinavian invaders, were taken over by the English. This assimilation of Norse words will be considered later when we look at characteristics of the Old English language.

King Alfred the Great

In the history of England and the English language it would be difficult to overestimate the importance of King Alfred the Great (849-899). From the time he became king in 871 until his death, he ruled the West Saxons in the area of Wessex in the southwestern part of England, while the Danes occupied the northeastern area known as the *Danelaw*. After stopping the expansion of the Danes into his kingdom, Alfred played a major role in preserving the literature and learning that had been threatened by the Viking invasions. During his reign, the English spoken by the West Saxons became the standard literary language; dialects spoken in other areas had little effect on written English at this time.

King Alfred ordered that schools be reestablished after the Viking threat subsided, and he saw to it that Latin documents were translated into English so that they would be available to those who could not read the original. Alfred himself learned Latin so that he could supervise the translation of works such as Bede's *Historia Ecclesiastica Gentis Anglorum* into the *History of the English Church and People*. It was also during Alfred's reign that the important historical record called the *Anglo-Saxon Chronicle* was begun.

Alfred's successors ruled England for more than a century until they were overwhelmed by renewed Viking raids in the eleventh century. England was actually ruled by Danish kings from 1017 until 1042, at which time Alfred's dynasty returned to the throne in the person of Edward the Confessor.

The Language

Anglo-Saxon Runes

Now that we have focused on some of the outside influences that affected the development of Old English, we turn to specific characteristics of the language itself.

As soon as they had established themselves in Britain, the *Engle* called their language **Englisc**, signifying the break with their homeland. For centuries the language of the Germanic tribes had been written with primitive symbols called **runes**. These symbols were understood by only a few priests and could not be read by most people. The Anglo-Saxon word *rūn* means "secret, mystery"; it also refers to any character in the runic alphabet. Runic symbols were used extensively for making inscriptions on pottery, jewelry, coins, and weapons. They were also used for memorial inscriptions on stone monuments, and some of these epitaphs contain examples of early Anglo-Saxon verse.

> The texts of the Anglo-Saxon rune-stones—as usual with Anglo-Saxon inscriptions—are not very exciting in content, but they present important records of the different local dia-

lects, since their geographical distribution is clear and they can often be dated on the basis of their sculptural decoration. (Page, 1987, p. 34)

The shape and number of runes varied from one location to the next, but a clear example of a version used in Britain was found in an inscription on a short sword (called a *scramasax*) found in the River Thames in the nineteenth century. The runes in this inscription are shown below.

f	u	þ	o	r	c	g	w	h	n	i	j	ė	p	x	s	t	b

e	ŋ (=ng)	d	l	m	œ	a	æ	y	êa

Anglo-Saxon Runic Alphabet (Elliott, 1963, p. 34)

This alphabet was called the **futhorc** after the first six symbols shown above. The third symbol, called the *thorn*, originally represented the voiceless sound of the letters *th* (as in *thin*). This symbol continued to be used even after the Latin alphabet was adopted in the seventh century because there was no symbol to represent *th* in the Latin language. Gradually it came to be used not only for voiceless *th* but also for voiced *th* (as in *there*) and was written Þ.

Germanic Basis of the English Language

We have referred to the language of the Anglo-Saxons and have pointed out that it formed the basis of the language we speak today. From now on we will use the term *Anglo-Saxon* to specify the Germanic tribes and the language they brought from their native land. The language that began to evolve in England after 449 A.D. will be called **Old English** (frequently abbreviated **OE**).

The most frequently used words in present-day English are of Anglo-Saxon origin. These are the vitally important function words we use to build sentences by showing relationships among other words. The spelling of some of these words has not changed at all since they first appeared in OE: *to, from, of, in, on, we,* and *is,* for example. The spelling of other words has changed, although the OE source is still evident: *ic* (I), *ēow* (you), *hēr* (here), *nama* (name), *hām* (home), *dōn* (do), *trēow* (tree), and *scip* (ship). Even though the English of today has been influenced by Latin, French, and other languages, it is firmly rooted in the Germanic speech of the Anglo-Saxons.

In addition to the function words of Germanic origin, many other important Old English words are still in use. A sampling of such words is given here, with each OE word followed by its modern spelling:

NOUNS	VERBS
frēond (friend)	etan (to eat)
cild (child)	drincan (to drink)
hūs (house)	libban (to live)
niht (night)	sēon (to see)
mōna (moon)	restan (to rest)
gēar (year)	singan (to sing)

Influence of the Latin Language and Alphabet

We have seen that Latin began to exert a strong influence on English when it was brought back by missionaries in the late sixth century. Our earliest written examples of the language date from about A.D. 700 and employ the Latin alphabet. The scribes who first wrote Old English used the symbols of their own language to represent the sounds they heard in a language that was new to them. This represents the first of many instances in which people who spoke another language were responsible for adapting their own concepts of sounds and symbols to the writing of English words.

The Anglo-Saxons adapted a number of Latin words such as *candela* (candle), *offerre* (offer), *regula* (rule), *ancora* (anchor), *planta* (plant), *circulus* (circle), and *schola* (school). This practice of absorbing words from other languages is most significant throughout the history of English. Such words were often changed in spelling and pronunciation to fit the characteristics of Anglo-Saxon, and this process continued for centuries as more and more foreign words entered the English language. Today our language contains many words that were taken from other languages and *Anglicized*—changed to fit the requirements of English speakers.

The Latin alphabet of the seventh century contained most of the letters we use today, although the shape of some characters differed from their present form, and the letters *q*, *x*, and *z* were rarely employed (Millward, 1989, p. 77). The letter *i* in the Latin alphabet, "besides being a vowel (as in *index*), had the consonant value of *y* (as in *major*, pronounced 'mayor')" (Diringer, 1977, p 62). The letter *j* was not originally found in the Latin alphabet but gradually evolved in the Middle Ages as an elongated form of the letter *i*. This letter *j* did not acquire the /j/ sound (as in *jump*) until the French language began to exert a strong influence following the Norman Conquest in 1066.

The letters *u*, *v*, and *w* have an interesting history as well. In Roman times the symbol *v* originally had the value of either the vowel *u* or the consonant *v*.

> Even in the later Roman monumental characters there appears only the sign **V**, having both the phonetic values *v* and *u*. At the same time, in the later Latin cursive documents, there is only the letter **U**, also employed indiscriminately for the sounds *u* and *v*. (Diringer, 1977, p. 74)

In English the letters *u* and *v* were used interchangeably even in the works of Shakespeare, where we find *have* spelled *haue* and *upon* spelled *vpon* in the First Folio of 1623. The practice of using *u* for the vowel and *v* for the consonant was not firmly established until the end of the seventeenth century.

The letter *w* did not appear until the eleventh century, when it was devised to represent a consonantal form of the letter *u*. It acquired the name *double u* because it was formed by joining two *v*s, the letter which had the value of *u* at that time. This character *vv* was employed by French scribes to represent an English sound that did not appear in their language (Diringer, 1977, p. 75).

Old Norse: The Language of the Vikings

The language of the Danes who began to invade Britain in the late eighth century was similar to that of the Anglo-Saxons. The two languages shared a common Germanic source and a number of words that were essentially the same in both: *man, wife, father, mother, house, bring, come, see, ride, stand,* and *sit,* for example. On the other hand, many words we use today are clearly derived from the Old Norse language of these Scandinavian invaders, particularly those words beginning with the /sk/ sound, such as *sky, skin, skirt, skill, score, scale,* and *scout.*

Some other present-day words that originated in Old Norse are nouns such as *bank, egg, guess, race, root, sister, window;* adjectives such as *awkward, loose, old, rugged, weak, wrong;* and verbs such as *call, drop, drown, give, lift, raise, scare,* and *scream.* The Danes also made other important contributions to the development of English: they brought the pronouns *they, them,* and *their;* they introduced the verb *are* to serve as the plural form for the verb *to be;* and they established the principle of using the inflection *-s* in the third person singular of verbs.

Some Characteristics of Old English Vocabulary

One striking feature of OE is its close relationship between sounds and symbols—much closer than is the case in English today. This can be seen in the words *why* and *where* which we now spell with *wh* but which actually have the /hw/ sound. In OE these words *did* begin with *hw:*

hwēol (wheel)	hwæt (what)	hwȳ (why)
hwæl (whale)	hwīl (while)	hwǣr (where)

All consonants were articulated in OE words such as *cniht* (youth), *sweord* (sword), and *wrītan* (to write). The letter *c* had the /k/ sound when followed by another consonant, and the *h* represented a breathy sound we no longer use. This explains why we now have many words in Modern English that contain "silent" letters: these words have retained vestiges of their Anglo-Saxon spellings long after their pronunciation changed.

Old English contained many compounds made up of words whose combined meanings suggested the meaning of the newly formed compound. Such self-explaining compounds are often found in present-day English *(hillside, snowstorm)* and have played an important role in Germanic languages. Usually the individual components gave a clear idea of the meaning of the compound word: the OE word for *helmet* was *hēafodbeorg* (head-protection), a lamp was called *lēohtfaet* (light-vessel), and the annual fair was called *gearmarcet* (year-market). A school was a *leorninghūs* (learning-house), and it is likely that the *leornere* (student, learner) of the tenth century was left with a splitting *hēafodece* (headache) after a day spent struggling with the complexities of the *Englisc* language.

When we look at Anglo-Saxon verse we will consider other compounds intended to create poetic images rather than to state literal descriptions. For now we mention only that the *sun*, in addition to being spelled *sunne*, could also be described more poetically as *daegcandel* (day-candle).

This method of forming compound words remains a feature of the German language today, which tends to combine familiar words to refer to a new object or concept and is less likely to adapt words from other languages. For example, the compound word *Unterseeboot* is formed from the German words *unter, See,* and *Boot*: this compound makes it clear that we are dealing with an *under-sea boat*. In English, such a vessel is called a *submarine*, a word formed from the Latin prefix *sub-*, meaning *under*, and the Latin root *mare*, meaning *sea* (which became the OE word *mere* and which we still use in words such as *mariner* and *maritime*).

Inflections in Old English

Another feature of Old English that sets it apart from the language we use today is *inflection*. Adjectives, nouns, and verbs were heavily inflected, using different endings or changing their spelling in other ways to show the function of these words within the sentence. (We retain a few of these OE inflections today to distinguish between singular and plural forms of nouns such as *man* and *men* or *mouse* and *mice*.)

The declension of nouns involved four cases, with either the internal spelling or the ending of the noun changed to indicate each case: *nominative* (to show that the word was used as the subject of a sentence); *accusative* (direct object); *dative* (indirect object); and *genitive* (to show possession). Furthermore, all nouns were ascribed a grammatical gender (masculine, feminine, or neuter), and adjectives had to agree with both the gender and the case of the noun they modified.

For example, if the noun *man* had been used as either the subject or direct object in a sentence ("The man is walking" or "I see the man"), its OE spelling would have been *mann*. If *man* were used as the indirect object ("Give the man his coat") then it would have been spelled *menn;* and if it showed possession ("This is the man's book"), the spelling would have been *mannes*. The plural required still more forms of the noun: *menn* as the plural subject or direct object of a sentence, *mannum* as the indirect object, and *manna* in the possessive case. This OE inflectional system was gradually simplified over the centuries, and most of the word-endings had all but disappeared by the time of Chaucer in the fourteenth century.

In present-day English we have a few inflections to indicate singular and plural nouns and to show the various forms of the verb, but in most cases these are the only inflections we need. The meaning of sentences today is determined by *word order*, not by inflections. We know that "The boy chases the dog" means one thing and "The dog chases the boy" means the opposite; the change of meaning is effected by the change in word order. In OE, different endings would have been required to show who was chasing whom.

Verbs also took many more forms in OE than they do today. The verb *healden* (to hold) had three forms for the singular: first person *healde*; second person *hieltst*; third person *hielt*. Other forms were used to show plurals, the past tense, and so on. Today we have a far more limited number of inflections to learn, and many of our verbs follow a single regular pattern (*look, looks, looked, looking*). Those verbs that are irregular (such as *see, saw, seen*) are often the ones that evolved from a Germanic rather than Latinic source.

Literature

Beowulf

Turning to a few examples of Old English literature, we pay particular attention to the significant body of verse composed during the period.

Perhaps the most famous example of Anglo-Saxon literature is the dramatic poem *Beowulf*, a heroic legend originally composed orally, possibly in the early eighth century, and written down at some later date. The poem was meant to be recited, and its language is rich with images conveying the feelings of bravery in battle and terror in the face of attacks by monsters. The *Beowulf* poet was a *scop* (bard, storyteller) who probably lived in the northern part of Britain (perhaps Mercia or Northumbria)—the language of the poem is more typical of the Angles of the north than of the Saxons living in southern Britain.

Beowulf is set in fifth- or sixth-century Sweden and Denmark and involves the Geats, a tribe living in southern Sweden. Some of the kings and tribes mentioned in it are known to have existed, although Beowulf himself is not encountered in any other document. The poem mixes legend with fact: the hero's adventures are drawn from folklore, and portions of the poem are similar to events recounted in Germanic history and legend of the period.

The poem begins with the funeral of Scyld Scefing, founder of the royal family of Denmark. The Danes have been decimated by the monster Grendel, who has been killing the warriors serving the Danish king Hrothgar. The young Beowulf, prince (*ætheling*) of the Geats, journeys from Sweden to Denmark and is able to kill not only the monster Grendel but also Grendel's mother, who lives in a cave at the bottom of a haunted lake. Beowulf returns to his native land where he becomes king (*cyning*) of the Geats. After ruling his people for fifty years, Beowulf is called upon to defend them against attacks by a fire-breathing dragon that has been roused to anger by a robber trying to steal the treasure-hoard guarded by the dragon. Both Beowulf and the dragon are killed in the final battle, and the poem ends with a prophecy of doom for the Geats at the hands of their enemies, the Swedes.

The following excerpt comes from the only surviving manuscript of *Beowulf,* copied around the year 1000. Although some letters are recognizable to the English reader of today, this writing seems foreign and we are not able to read it without help. Following the scrap of manuscript, the passage is reproduced in modern type, with a translation into present-day English placed beside it.

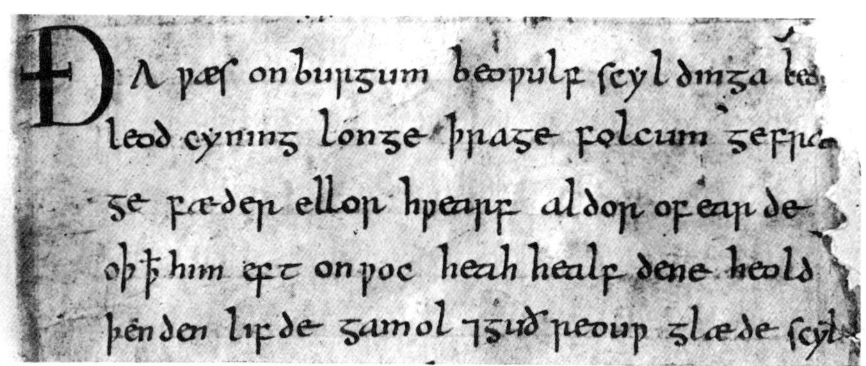

(McCrum *et al.,* 1986, p. 72)

Đā wæs on burgum   [*Bēow*] Scyldinga | Then in the strongholds   [Beow] the Scylding
lēo*f* lēod-cyning   longe þrāge | was king of all Denmark,   beloved by his people,
folcum gefrǣge   —fæder ellor hwearf | famous a long time   —his noble father
aldor of earde—   oþþæt him eft onwōc | having passed away—   had a son in his turn,
hēah Healfdene;   hēold þenden lifde, | Healfdene the great,   who, while he lived,
gamol ond gūð-rēouw,   glæde Scyldingas. | aged, war-fierce,   ruled lordly Scyldings.

(Chickering, 1977, pp. 50-51)

This passage shows that some runic symbols were retained even after the adoption of the Latin alphabet. You can see the *thorn* (þ), used to represent the voiceless *th* (as in *thin*); a capital *thorn* appears at the beginning of the excerpt. Another symbol, the *eth* (ð), represented the voiced *th* (as in *then*). Also, the letters *a* and *e* were joined in a single ligature to form the *ash* (æ) representing the *short a* sound. A few other symbols differing from the Latin alphabet were also retained, but the three mentioned here are the ones we encounter most often.

Characteristics of Old English Verse

Old English verse employed a great many **synonyms** to refer to particularly important people or objects. In Beowulf at least three dozen words all refer to the *prince,* including the word *cniht,* which originally meant a *young man* in Anglo-Saxon and evolved into the concept of the *knight* in the age of chivalry. The *hero* is also called *eorl* (chief, nobleman), *rinc* or *wiga* (warrior), or *ealdor* (leader, king). The *sea* was of great importance to the Anglo-Saxons: the many synonyms for it included *flōd* (flood, wave), *mere* (sea, lake), and *brim* (wave, water).

Closely related to these synonyms are **kennings**, metaphorical compound words used to provide a variety of images. The *king* might be praised as *landfruma* (ruler of the land), *līffrēa* (life-lord), or *wuldres wealdend* (ruler of glory). The *sea* could be described more colorfully as *hronrād* (the whale's riding-place), *garsecg* (encircling ocean), or *swanrād* (the swan's riding-place). A *ship* (OE *scip*) could be called *godne gegyrwan* (a good wave-rider). These and many more *kennings* brought power and vigor to Anglo-Saxon verse, providing the *scop* with a wealth of colorful descriptions to hold the attention of his audience.

Old English verse did not employ the type of end rhyme that we find so often in more recent poetry, and its meter was defined by patterns of stress, not by length of vowels or by number of syllables. Closely allied with the patterns of stress was the use of **alliteration**, the repetition of the same initial sound in two or more words in a line of poetry.

> The Old English poetic line has two halves, divided by a sharp pause, or caesura. There are two beats to each half-line. Thus there are four beats to the line. The alliteration of the whole line is determined by the first heavily stressed syllable of the second half-line. This third stress will alliterate with either or both of the two stresses in the first half-line. The third stress is the key sound that locks the two half-lines together. (Chickering, 1977, p. 29)

All the features described by Chickering can be found in the beginning of a poem entitled *The Ruin.*

THE RUIN

Wrætlic is þes wealstan,
    wyrde gebræcon;
burgstede burston,
    brosnað enta geweorc.
Hrofas sind gehrorene,
    hreorge torras,
hrungeat berofen, hrim on lime,
scearde scurbeorge scorene,
    gedrorene,
ældo undereotone.

Well-wrought this wall:
Wierds broke it.
The stronghold burst....

Snapped rooftrees, towers fallen,
the work of the Giants,
the stonesmiths, mouldereth.

Rime scoureth gatetowers
rime on mortar.

Shattered the showershields,
roofs ruined,
age under-ate them.

(Alexander, 1970, pp. 30-31)

The first line is given below, with the four stressed syllables indicated by number:

Wrætlic is þes wealstan,   wyrde gebræcon;
1   2   3   4

The *w* on the third stress is alliterated in the first and second as well, while the final stressed syllable does not match the alliterative pattern. The word *gebræcon* begins with a prefix (*ge-*), placing the stress on the following syllable.

Students can find the remaining alliteration, taking into account that the words *gehrorene* in line three and *berofen* in line four also begin with prefixes that shift the stress to the following syllable.

The Anglo-Saxon Chronicle

During the reign of King Alfred in the late ninth century, monks began to keep a historical record of events. We cannot be sure that the king was directly involved in this project, but his encouragement of learning certainly provided a good environment for the undertaking. This historical record, called the *Anglo-Saxon Chronicle*, consists of seven different documents: taken together, they provide a record of events from the Year One through the coronation of King Henry II in 1154. The monks had to rely on earlier sources of varying reliability to provide information on events before the middle of the ninth century, but from the time of King Alfred until the middle of the twelfth century, the chronicle gives a first-hand account of events as they happened. The *Anglo-Saxon Chronicle* provides an important historical record and is also one of the earliest and most important works of prose in Old English.

The following example, taken from the *Peterborough Chronicle* (one of the documents included in the *Anglo-Saxon Chronicle*), shows how OE was written in the late eleventh century. Following the original manuscript is a version written in modern script, with a translation into present-day English given below. The year is written in red in the original manuscript and is barely discernible here. The first word, an abbreviated form of *Millesimo*, means *one thousand* and is followed by the Roman numerals lxxvi, yielding the date 1076. The abbreviation for the word *and* looks much like the numeral 7; it is used in the original and in the version in modern script.

(Whitelock, 1954, p. 121)

Mill*esi*mo lxxvi. On þisu*m* geare forðferde Swægn cyng on Dænmercan, 7 Harold his sunu feng to ᛁþeᛁ kynerice. 7 Se cyng geaf Westmynster Vithele abbode se wæs ær abb*ot* on Bærnege. 7 Walþeof eorl ᛁwesᛁ beheafdod on Winceastre, 7 his lic wearð gelead to Crulande. 7 Se cyng for ofer sæ 7 lædde his fyrde to Brytlande 7 beset þone castel Dol; 7 þa Bryttas hine heoldon þ*et* se cyng co*m* of Francland; 7 Willelm þanon for 7 þær forleas ægðer ge men ge hors 7 feola his gersuma.

(Clark, 1970, p. 6)

1076 In this year Swein, king of Denmark, died, and Harold, his son, succeeded to the realm. And the king gave Westminster to Abbot Vitalis who had been abbot of Bernay. And Earl Waltheof was beheaded at Winchester; and his body was taken to Crowland. And the king went overseas and led his force to Brittany and besieged the castle at Dol; and the Bretons held it until the king came from France, and William went away and lost there both men and horses and much of his treasure. (Whitelock, 1961, p. 158)

The original version can be compared with the modern translation to form a demonstration text for students. They can find readily identifiable words such as *on*, *his*, *to*, *men*, and *for* in order to see the frequency with which these words were used even at this early period. They might also see that some words are recognizable even though spelled differently from present-day English: *cyng* (king), *sunu* (son), and *castel* (castle), for example. Students can begin to gain an idea of the great differences between Old English and present-day English by comparing and discussing these excerpts.

Old English reached its final stage of development some two hundred years after the reign of Alfred the Great. The next important event in the history of English was to come with the introduction of yet another language into Britain near the end of the eleventh century.

Summary

Although many function words are derived from Old English and other words have been handed down somewhat changed in spelling and pronunciation, it is important to remember that this language is based on a structural system very different from that found in the English of today.

> Old English was a synthetic language with a fairly well-developed range of inflections. The point is worth emphasizing because once we have acquired a little Old English we recognize the precursors of many of our modern words and constructions, and that sense of the difference between Old and Modern English begins to diminish; we stop considering how the attitudes which speakers of a synthetic language have towards their language may differ from our own. Yet if we learn an inflected language like modern German we never feel, however well we come to know it, that we grasp all the nuances within its literature, partly because speakers of an inflected language have different expectations. (Blake, 1977, p. 34)

Old English, so different from the language we speak today, did produce a body of verse that is significant for what it tells us about the Germanic heritage of the first *Englisc* people and for its eloquence and power in recounting the fierce battles and heroic deeds of these people. The use of Old English for prose began some time after the first works of verse, and much of the prose we have today exists because of the efforts of King Alfred the Great. The king himself, through his own translations of historical and philosophical works from Latin, was largely responsible for establishing the tradition of Old English prose carried on by later scholars and ecclesiastics until the time of the Norman Conquest in the late eleventh century. "So large and varied a body of literature, in verse and prose, gives ample testimony to the universal competence, at times to the power and beauty, of the Old English language" (Baugh and Cable, 1978, p. 70).

Exercises

The following exercises are included here to show how students may work with the words of Old English after they have been introduced to the history and literature of the period. Instructions for the student and the exercises themselves are given on the next four pages; answers and other suggestions for the teacher are given on a separate page following the exercises. Feel free to make multiple copies of the student exercises if you want to use them in your classes.

Old English: Exercises

1. Spelling

Look at these Old English words and write their present-day spellings. Remember that the infinitive of OE verbs often ended with *-an*. Also, in OE the letter ā had the sound in the modern word *father*. Over the centuries, pronunciation changed so that many words spelled with ā in OE now have the /ō/ sound in *grow*.

1. bedd _______________________________

2. etan _______________________________

3. scip _______________________________

4. glof _______________________________

5. stān _______________________________

6. mann _______________________________

7. helpan _______________________________

8. snāw _______________________________

9. drincan _______________________________

10. mūs _______________________________

Old English: Exercises

2. Compound Words

Look at the individual OE words listed below and then look at the compounds formed from them. Determine the meaning of the compound words and write them with modern spellings.

Individual OE Words

boga (bow)   *mon* (man)   *scīma* (light, brightness)

sunna (sun)   *rēn* (rain)   *flota* (fleet of ships)

dæg (day)   *gebland* (confusion, storm)

OE Compound Words

1. rēnboga ________________________________

2. sunnanscīma ___________________________

3. flotmon _______________________________

4. snāwgebland ___________________________

5. Sunnandæg _____________________________

Old English: Exercises

3. Suffixes

Some Old English suffixes are similar to those we use today. Look at the OE suffixes and base words given below and then write the modern version of the OE words containing these suffixes. You can easily figure out some words that are close to Modern English (*cild = child*, for example).

OE Suffixes:

-had: similar to our *-hood*, meaning a condition or quality (*likelihood*) or a time or period (*boyhood*).

-nes: same as our *-ness*, meaning a state, condition, or quality (*kindness, happiness*)

OE Base Words:

hefig (heavy) *modig* (proud) *cniht* (boy)

OE Words with Suffixes:

1. hefignes _______________________________

2. cildhad _______________________________

3. modignes _______________________________

4. falsehad _______________________________

5. stilnes _______________________________

6. cnihthad _______________________________

Old English: Exercises

4. Translation

Look at the following entries from the *Anglo-Saxon Chronicle* for the years 488 and 556 and use the glossaries to make your own translation of each sentence. Then compare your translations with the Modern English versions marked A and B below. After each translation, indicate the year that is being discussed. The important thing is not to guess the year but to look at each sentence in the original and get some sense of how the language was used more than a thousand years ago.

Original Versions in the *Anglo-Saxon Chronicle*

488 Hēr AEsc fēng to rīce and wæs xxiii wintra Cantwara cyning.

> **Glossary:** Hēr (in this year)
> AEsc (an Anglo-Saxon chief)
> fēng to rīce (ascended the throne)
> Cantwara (people of Kent)
> cyning (king)

556 Hēr Cynric and Ceawlin fuhton with Brettas æt Beran byrg.

> **Glossary:** fuhton (fought)
> Brettas (the Britons)
> Beran byrg (Barbury Castle)

Modern Translations

A. In this year Cynric and Ceawlin fought against the Britons at Barbury castle. (Year _______________)

B. In this year AEsc ascended to the throne and was king of the people of Kent for 23 years. (Year _______________)

Answers to Old English Exercises

1. Spelling

1. bed	6. man
2. to eat	7. to help
3. ship	8. snow
4. glove	9. to drink
5. stone	10. mouse

Students can see the use of doubled consonants at the end of short-vowel words (*bedd, mann*). This changed to the CVC principle (Consonant-Vowel-Consonant) centuries later. Verbs were inflected to show the infinitive (*-an* in this case); we now use *to*, and drop the inflection. The *sc* pattern had the /sh/ sound in OE, and other consonants and vowels have changed in modern spellings of words such as *glof* and *snāw*.

2. Compound Words

1. rainbow	4. snowstorm
2. sunshine	5. Sunday
3. sailor (literally "fleet-man")	

Point out to students that some words in OE had more than one spelling, just as OE had a number of words for the same thing in many cases. They should not be surprised to find *man* spelled *mann* in one place and *mon* in another. Variations in spelling can also result from inflections.

3. Suffixes

1. heaviness, weight	4. falsehood
2. childhood	5. stillness, quiet
3. pride (literally "proudness")	6. boyhood, youth

4. Translation

A. 556   B. 488

Some individual words and short phrases in OE may need to be translated as longer phrases: For example, *xxiii wintra* means *for 23 winters,* and *Cantwara* means *the people of Kent.*

Middle English
(c. 1100 – 1500)

External History

The Norman Invasion

In the year 1066, England was invaded and occupied once again by foreigners who brought still another language into the island. These invaders came from *Normandy*, the area along the coast of France just across the channel from southern England. The people were called *Normans* and were led by William the Conqueror, whose army defeated the forces of the English under King Harold Godwineson at the Battle of Hastings. The map on page 30 shows the route of the Normans across the channel to the southeast coast of England.

The Normans or *Norsemen* (Northmen) were originally Vikings from Denmark and Norway. They began their raids along the coast of France during the ninth century, at the same time as other Viking tribes were harassing much of Britain. By the tenth century the Norsemen in France had settled near the mouth of the River Seine in the area that was to become *Normandy*, the land of the Normans.

We have seen that the Old Norse language of the Vikings sprang from the same source as the Germanic language of the Anglo-Saxons, a fact which enabled these two groups to communicate with each other in England as their languages merged to form Old English. On the other hand, the Norsemen who settled in France did not retain their Scandinavian speech. They adopted the language of their new homeland and thus came to speak an early form of **French**, a Romance language rooted in

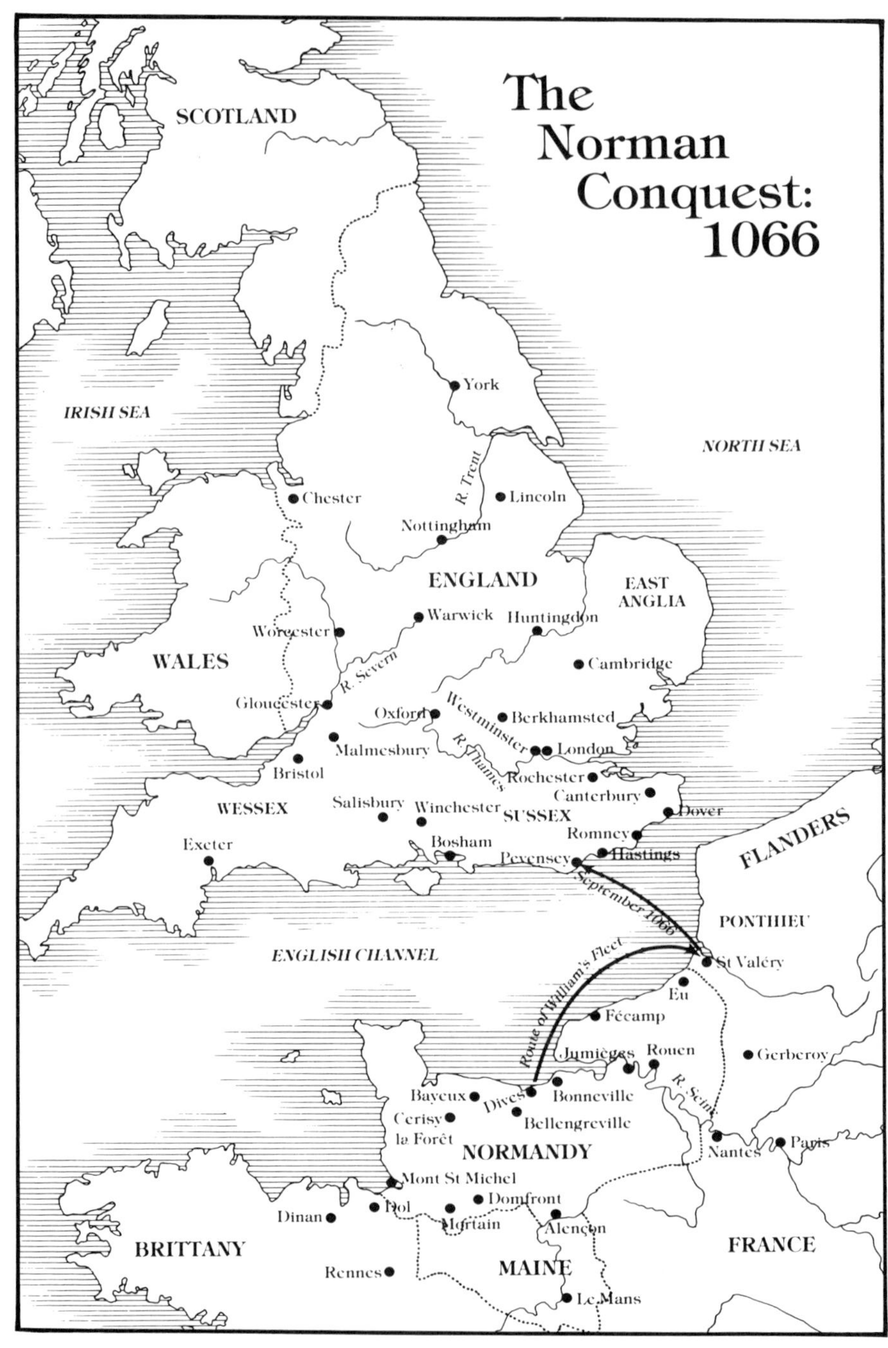

Route of the Normans into England (Savage, 1983, p. 192)

Latin. This Romance language differed in important ways from the Germanic language of the English, and the interaction between Norman French and Old English was a strong motivating force in the development of Middle English from the late eleventh century up until the appearance of the first printing presses in England in the late fifteenth century.

Influence of the Normans in England

The Normans who first occupied England spoke only their native French. This practice was entirely agreeable to King William, a man not noted for his interest in higher learning.

> The Conqueror was totally illiterate and the one dubious story that he tried to learn the speech of his new subjects admits that he failed. On the other hand the autograph crosses with which he authenticated documents make him the first English king who is known to have handled a pen. (Baker, 1966, pp. 214-215)

French was the language of the court and of society, while Latin continued as the language of official documents, of international diplomacy, and of the church. The English people, on the other hand, continued to speak their native language and adapted those French words that seemed most useful. As time went on, the interacting languages and cultures of the French and English eventually yielded the mixture of Anglo-Saxon, Norman French, and Latin that formed the language we now call **Middle English (ME)**.

Although French supplanted English as the written language of England during the twelfth century, its influence began to decline in the thirteenth century because the English kings lost control of their French provinces, and the two countries became more and more isolated from each other. By the time Chaucer began his literary work in the latter half of the fourteenth century, the French language in England had been cut off from its source, and its use became more and more restricted to the nobility and those with higher education. Gradually the French language in England came to be used by only a few of the nobility and the educated classes. French had become a language "that had ceased to be the mother-tongue of anybody and had always to be taught" (Pope, 1934, p. 424).

The Language

French Additions to the English Lexicon

The addition of French words to the English language became increasingly important after the Norman victory in 1066.

> Although this influx of French words was brought about by the victory of the Conqueror and by the political and social consequences of that victory, it was neither sudden nor immediately apparent. Rather it began slowly and continued with varying tempo for a long time. Indeed it can hardly be said to have ever stopped. (Baugh and Cable, 1978, p. 167)

Among the most important French contributions are words relating to government, law, and the arts. Some words that apply to government include *president, parliament, congress, administer, court, council, authority,* and even *government* itself. Legal terms include *justice, crime, defendant, plaintiff,* and *evidence,* while words relating to the arts include *sculpture, painting, color, image, poet, tragedy, prologue,* and *figure.*

In some cases, French words were added to supplement already existing English words in a particular area. For example, English words for the nobility included *king, queen, earl,* and *knight*; to these were added the French *duke, marquis,* and *baron.* The English language provided the words *town, hall, house,* and *home*; French added *city, village, palace,* and *mansion.* In other cases, English words expressing concrete concepts are matched by near-synonyms in French expressing more abstract ideas: English *freedom* and French *liberty*; *love* and *affection*; *hatred* and *enmity*; *truth* and *veracity*; and so on.

Of the many other English words that have been adapted from French, a few familiar ones are these:

Nouns	Adjectives	Verbs
action	brief	advise
adventure	certain	allow
country	clear	arrange
force	courteous	carry
honor	cruel	conceal

Nouns	Adjectives	Verbs
marriage	foreign	destroy
mountain	gentle	furnish
number	original	observe
piece	principal	practice
quality	secret	receive
reason	special	remember
spirit	subtle	surprise

Students might look for these words in a collegiate or un-abridged dictionary to find the original form. It would be a good idea to have them consult an English-French dictionary as well. Even though some of the words are spelled the same in French as in English (*force* and *cruel*, for example), one must keep in mind the differences in pronunciation between the two languages. In the case of words with suffixes, advise your students to consult the dictionary entry for the base word: for example, *action* (see *act*); *original* (see *origin*). This dictionary work will also allow students to discover the Latin form of many French words (as, for example, *special* from Old French *especial*, from Latin *specialis*, meaning "individual, particular"; also related to the word *species*).

Adapting French Words to the English Language

Throughout history, English words (like their Germanic predecessors) have been spoken with a strong stress on the stem, a stress that is retained even when affixes and other elements are involved. For example, the OE word *turnian* (to turn, revolve) forms the basis for words we use today such as TURN, TURN-ing, TURN-er, re-TURN-able, and TURN-pike. French words, on the other hand, usually have a slight stress on the final syllable. Consequently, native English speakers altered the spelling and pronunciation of many French words to make them fit the characteristics of spoken English, just as they had done with words brought by the Danes many years before.

For example, the French word *pouvoir* (pou-VOIR) became the English word *power*, with emphasis on the first syllable.

Other changes in spelling and pronunciation can be seen in French words such as *hôte*, *côte*, and *hôpital*, which became the English *host*, *coast*, and *hospital*; and in *couleur* (color), *compter* (to count), *expliquer* (to explain), *fleur* (flower), and *histoire* (history).

So long as they relied on the spoken word, it was possible for Englishmen and Normans to get along with a language that mixed Old English with words from French and Latin. When the language came to be written, however, it was more difficult to manage because some sounds in OE were not matched by letters in the Latin alphabet, and there were no standard spellings for many words. These problems began to be resolved by the fourteenth century, but it was not until printing was introduced into England in the late fifteenth century that the need for consistent spelling conventions became apparent to all.

Changes in Old English Inflections and Pronunciation

An important feature of Middle English was the marked simplification of the inflectional system that had been used in the Germanic language of the Anglo-Saxons. Most inflected forms of OE nouns, adjectives, and verbs were dropped in ME as the structure of the language changed to make *word order* the determining factor. This development, one of the most significant in the entire history of the language, paved the way for the system of grammar that we use today.

Simplification of the inflectional system from Old English to Middle English can be seen most clearly in adjectives, which not only had to match the four cases of nouns in OE but also required different endings for the three genders as well. Listed below are the inflections required in OE for the adjective *hard* in the masculine gender only; even more endings were needed to form the feminine and neuter genders.

Old English	*Singular*	*Plural*
Nominative:	heard	hearde
Accusative:	heardne	hearde
Genitive:	heardes	heardra
Dative:	heardum	heardum

By the fourteenth century, the declension of this word *for all cases* in ME had been reduced to *hard* for the singular and *harde* for the plural. All other inflections had disappeared, and even the plural inflection was eventually dropped for adjectives.

Pronunciation also changed as inflections became less important. For example, OE words such as *nama* (name), *mete* (meat), and *wicu* (week) originally contained clearly pronounced short-vowel sounds in both syllables. (Old English *short e* and *short i* had essentially the same sounds that they have today in *set* and *sit*, but *short a* had the sound of the modern word *swap*, and *short u* had the sound of the modern word *put*.) By the fourteenth century the spelling of some of these words had changed (*nama* to *name, wicu* to *weke*), and the final vowel no longer played the important role that it did when the language was inflected. Instead, this final vowel took on the sound of the *schwa* in ME and was spelled *e* in each case. Even the *schwa* sound gradually disappeared by the early fifteenth century. This trend toward lengthening the sound of the first vowel while weakening the sound of the final vowel led to a marked change in the pronunciation of English by the time of Shakespeare.

Literature

Geoffrey Chaucer (c. 1340-1400)

Perhaps the most significant literary figure in fourteenth-century England, Geoffrey Chaucer was the first to use Middle English to compose literary works of major importance. His writings also did much to establish the speech of London as the standard for the English language. Dialects spoken in other regions of the country became less important as the language moved gradually toward a single standard form based on London English.

Chaucer's most famous poetic work, the *Canterbury Tales*, tells of a group of people traveling from London to Canterbury near the southeast coast of England. Even though some words are unfamiliar to us today, we can read much of Chaucer's poetry without extreme difficulty. On page 36 is the beginning of Chaucer's description of a knight who was among the travelers to Canterbury. The excerpt is from the Hengwrt manuscript, copied about 1400-1410 shortly after Chaucer's death:

> A knyght ther was, and that a worthy man,
> That fro the tyme that he first bigan
> To ryden out, he loued chiualrye,
> Trouthe and honour, fredom and curteisye.

These lines are an example of Middle English spelling near the end of the fourteenth century. The letter *y* was often used where we would write the letter *i*, and the letter *u* was still used to represent the consonant *v* in words such as *loue*. Students should be able to transcribe this passage fairly easily into present-day English:

> A knight there was, and that a worthy man,
> That from the time that he first began
> To ride out, he loved chivalry,
> Truth and honor, freedom and courtesy.

The following example, also taken from the Hengwrt manuscript, shows how Chaucer's language was written in his own day. Below the facsimile, the same passage is given in modern script, followed a few lines below by a version in present-day English. The short diagonal lines or *virgules* (/) in the original are used to indicate syntactic breaks, much as commas are used today. This excerpt is from "The Clerk of Oxenforde," now usually called "The Clerk's Tale." (In Chaucer's day, a *clerk* was a scholar who had attended a university and had also been admitted to a religious order; the modern word *cleric* is related.)

> ¶And whan this Walter / saw hir pacience
> Hir glad cheere / and no malice at al
> And he so ofte / had doon to hir*e* offence
> And she ay sad / and constant as a wal
> Continuynge eu*ere* / hir Innocence ouer al
> This sturdy Markys / gan his herte dresse
> To rewen / vp on hir wifly stedfastnesse

(Ruggiers, 1979, p. 749)

Although the meaning of this passage can be fully under-stood only within the context of the complete story of Walter and Griselda, the excerpt does allow students to see how English looked in the fourteenth century. They should be able to make sense of the language if they are given help on words such as *ofte* (often), *doon* (done), *hire* (her), *ay* (ever, always), *gan* (began), *dresse* (to address), and *rewen* (to have pity). They might even attempt their own transcription into present-day English before looking at this more free rendition:

> And now, when Walter saw her happy face,
> Her patience, with no rancour there at all,
> However often he had done her mischief,
> She stood as firm and steadfast as a wall,
> Continuing in innocence through all,
> His obdurate heart inclined to take pity
> Upon Griselda's wifely constancy. (Wright, 1985, p. 308)

The Publications of William Caxton

Although French remained the official language of the English king and his court even during Chaucer's lifetime, it ceased to be so in 1415, when Henry V began using English in official documents and proclaimed it the only language of England from that time on. Middle English is found in the books published in the late fifteenth century by William Caxton (c. 1422-1491), who set up the first printing press in London in 1476. He not only published Chaucer and other English writers but also translated writings from French into English. Like Chaucer, Caxton used London English in his work, thus further establishing it as the standard for the English language.

The following passage gives an idea of the difficulty Caxton encountered in dealing with the unsettled state of the language in his day:

> Certaynly it is harde to playse every man by cause of dyversite
> & chaunge of langage. For in these days every man that is in
> ony reputacyon in his countre, wyll utter his commynycacyon
> and maters in suche maners & termes that fewe men shall
> understonde theym. (Blake, 1973, p. 80)

In this excerpt, students can see how the language looked as it moved from Middle English into the period of Early Modern English. Spellings appear strange to us in some cases, but it is easier to read this passage than it is to read *Beowulf* or some passages in Chaucer. You may want to have students write this passage in present-day English:

> Certainly it is hard to please every man because of diversity and change of language. For in these days every man that is in any reputation in his country, will utter his communication and matters in such manners and terms that few men shall understand them.

One of Caxton's first publications in England was the story of King Arthur as told by Sir Thomas Malory, who was born early in the fifteenth century and lived until 1471. Malory's *Le Morte Darthur (The Death of Arthur)* was composed in the 1460s and shows how Middle English appeared in its late stages. The first example below shows the beginning of the story as printed by Caxton, followed by the same passage printed in modern type.

℩ Capitulum primum

Jt befel in the dayes of Wther pendragon when he was kynge of all Englond / and so regned that there was a myghty duke in Cornewaill that helde warre ageynst hym long tyme / And the duke was called the duke of Tyntagil / and so by meanes kynge Wther send for this duk / chargyng hym to brynge his wyf with hym / for she was called a fair lady / and a passynge wyse / and her name was called Jgrayne /

(Caxton, 1485)

IT befel in the dayes of Vther Pendragon, when he was Kynge of all Englond and so regned, that there was a myghty duke in Cornewaill that helde warre ageynst hym long tyme, and the duke was called the Duke of Tyntagil. And so by meanes Kynge Vther send for this duk, chargyng hym to brynge his wyf with hym, for she was called a fair lady and a passynge wyse, and her name was called Igrayne.

(Spisak, 1983, p. 33)

As with the excerpt from Chaucer's *Canterbury Tales*, the virgule is used as punctuation in the original; commas and periods are employed in the version in modern script. The most noticeable features are the spelling of the first word *Hit* for *It*, the use of *y* in many cases in which we would use *i*, and the use of *V* instead of *U* at the beginning of the name *Vther Pendragon*. Students should be able to render a version in present-day English:

> It befell in the days of Uther Pendragon, when he was King of all England and so reigned, that there was a mighty duke in Cornwall that held war against him for a long time, and the duke was called the Duke of Tintagel. And so by means King Uther sent for this duke, charging him to bring his wife with him, for she was called a fair lady and a passing wise, and her name was called Igraine.

With the growing availability of books following the introduction of printing in the late fifteenth century, people began to become increasingly aware of the unsettled state of English spelling and grammar. As we move into the period of Early Modern English, we will see what measures were taken to establish spelling conventions and standards of usage which would reconcile all the varied influences that had affected the language since its beginnings.

Changes in the Language during the Period of Middle English

Although most of the examples we have seen are from Chaucer and Caxton, their writings actually represent a relatively late stage in the development of Middle English. English all but ceased to be written for more than a century after the Norman Conquest, and after that it was often written by Norman French scribes who interpreted English in terms of their own language and spelling conventions. The extent of change in the English language during the period of Middle English can be seen in the next two examples, written some 250 years apart.

The first passage is from the early twelfth century and is found in the *Peterborough Chronicle*, one of the portions of the *Anglo-Saxon Chronicle* that continued to be written after the Norman Conquest. Mossé explains the state of the English language in the twelfth century:

> At this period the older literary and orthographic traditions were still known, but they no longer had the same force. The scribe tried to reproduce as faithfully as possible the language spoken in his time and in his region. Thus he writes an early

Middle English of the central north-east, but the syntax is confused, and the notation of the forms and the sounds, which seems to follow no method, is rather uncertain. (Mossé, 1952, p. 133)

A portion of the entry from the *Peterborough Chronicle* for the year 1137 is given below, followed by a modern version.

M*illesimo* cxxx*ι*vii*ι*. Ðis gære for þe *ι*king*ι* Steph*ne* ofer sæ to Normandi; 7 ther wes underfangen, forþi ðat hi uuenden ðat he sculde ben alsuic alse the e*om* wes, 7 for he hadde get his tresor; ac he todeld it 7 scatered sotlice. Micel hadde Henri *king* gadered gold 7 syluer, 7 na god ne dide me for his saule tharof.

(Clark, 1970, p. 55)

1137. This year King Stephen went overseas to Normandy, and was received there because they expected that he would be just as his uncle had been, and because he still had his treasure; but he distributed it and squandered it like a fool. King Henry had gathered a great amount—gold and silver—and no good to his soul was done with it. (Whitelock, 1961, p. 198)

A later example from the year 1386 is of both historical and literary interest. It is the beginning of a petition by a *mercer* (a merchant dealing in textiles) who asked Parliament to redress the wrongs done to him. The petition appears in the *Rotuli Parliamentorum* (*Rolls of Parliament*), the records kept from 1278 until 1503 consisting mostly of public and private petitions to Parliament and the answers to them.

Leafing through the *Rotuli Parliamentorum*, a person will find nothing but Latin and Anglo-Norman until, suddenly, in 1386 he runs onto this petition in English, drawn up by the Mercers. . . . It is necessary to wait until the beginning of the 15th century to see the use of English extended into these official acts. (Mossé, 1952, pp. 282-83)

The mercer's petition is given here in the original:

To the moost noble and Worthiest Lordes, moost ryghtful and wysest conseille to owre lige Lorde the Kyng, compleynen, if it like to yow, the folk of the Mercerye of London as a membre of the same citee, of many wronges subtiles and also open oppressions, y-do to hem by longe tyme here bifore passed.

In literal Modern English this passage reads as follows:

> To the most noble and worthiest lords, most rightful and wisest counsel to our liege lord the king, complain, if it please you, the folk of the mercers of London as a member of the same city, of many subtle wrongs and also open oppression, done to them for a long time here before past.

Look back at the entry in the *Peterborough Chronicle* for 1137 and compare it with the version of the mercer's petition of 1386. You can see how much the language changed in a relatively short period.

The fourteenth-century words listed below still look familiar to us today, but the meaning of each has changed significantly since Chaucer's day. You can see how easily we might get the wrong impression if all Middle English words were read as though they had Modern English meanings.

axe was a form of the verb "to ask," not a chopping tool

barn meant "child" ("bairn"), not a place for cows

free meant "noble, generous" as well as "free"

raged meant "white with frost"

space meant "moment, time" (*in space* meant "right away")

spellinge meant "story"

Summary

Before moving on to Early Modern English, we should stop for a moment to review some of the most significant features of Middle English. In particular, we need to remember that the written tradition of Old English, embodied in the work of the scribes and scholars who flourished from the time of King Alfred until the Norman Conquest, all but disappeared in the twelfth century as French became the dominant written language in England. When English began to reemerge in the late thirteenth century, it was often written by Norman scribes who approached the language in terms of the sounds and spellings of Norman French. This added one more outside influence to the English language, much as the Roman scribes of the eighth century had approached Old English in terms of their knowledge of Latin.

Even though the printed language of Chaucer or Caxton may look a bit more accessible to us than does Old English, the *sound* of Middle English is closer to that of Old English than it is to the language we speak today. Furthermore, many words we still use today had different meanings in Middle English. This may lead us to misunderstand or distort our interpretation of Middle English by reading current meanings into some words because they look similar to those we use now.

> When Chaucer says of the Knight in the General Prologue to the *Canterbury Tales* that "he loved *chivalrye*, / *Trouthe* and honour, *fredom* and *curteisie*"; that he was "ful *worthy* in his lordes werre"; that "*therto* had he *riden*, no man ferre"; . . . not one of the italicized words means quite what it means today. (Clark, 1967, p. 112)

We can see the difference between Chaucer's vocabulary and current usage in words such as *chivalrye* (also often spelled *chevalerie*): in the fourteenth century, this word referred to a host of armored mounted warriors (French *cheval* means *horse*), not just to gallant, courteous behavior. *Curteisie* meant politeness and good manners in Chaucer's day, but it also referred to the whole complex of courtly ideals associated with *chivalrye*. *Fredom* carried several meanings in addition to the idea of individual liberty: it could also mean nobility of character, a special privilege (such as the right to buy or sell property), or a king's authority. The verb *riden* meant not only to ride on horseback but more specifically to set out in search of adventure (*riden oute*), to be part of a military group in battle, or to ride in a procession. It could also mean to sail in a ship or to "ride at anchor," and could even mean to move quickly or to become disturbed.

The examples we have cited should give some idea of the dynamic growth of English from the twelfth century, when the language of Wessex was eclipsed by Norman French, until the fifteenth century, when the language of Chaucer's London became available to all in the books of Caxton and other printers. The following review brings into focus some of the prominent characteristics of Middle English:

- First, during this period the leveling of inflections begun in the closing stages of Old English was completed.

- Second, dialect differences were further reduced so that the future history of London English became that of British English as a whole.

- Third, in this evolutionary state of the language the principles of word order put the final touches upon a functionally analytic syntax; future developments were merely stylistic refinements.

- Fourth, Late Middle English supported a phonetic instability that led to the Great Vowel Shift, the silencing of certain consonants, and the phonemic transmutation of others. This phonetic instability was the progenitor of Early Modern English. (Nist, 1966, pp. 172-73)

Middle English: Exercises

1. Spelling

Look at the following words as spelled in Old English (OE) and in Middle English (ME) and then write the Modern English spelling. Remember that infinitives in OE and ME often end with *-an* or *-en*.

OE	ME	Modern English
1. dohtor	doughter	__________________
2. findan	finden	__________________
3. leornian	lernen	__________________
4. nefa	nevew	__________________
5. cēpan	kepen	__________________
6. heorte	herte	__________________

Middle English: Exercises

2. Words Used by Chaucer

Look at the following words from Chaucer and write their modern spellings.

1. battailles _________________________________

2. biginne _________________________________

3. bisyde _________________________________

4. coude _________________________________

5. foughten _________________________________

6. in stede _________________________________

7. sesoun _________________________________

8. tyme _________________________________

Middle English: Exercises

3. Loanwords from French

The following French words were absorbed into English with only slight changes in spelling, although pronunciation often differed noticeably. Write the present-day English spelling for each French word.

French   **English**

1. actif   ______________________________

2. musique   ______________________________

3. papier   ______________________________

4. sujet   ______________________________

5. jugement   ______________________________

6. personne   ______________________________

Middle English: Exercises

4. Vocabulary

The French words words below have changed noticeably in their English forms. Write the English words and explain briefly what changes have been made in spelling and treatment of inflections (either altered or eliminated). Remember that many French verbs end with *-er* or *-re* in the infinitive.

French	English	Changes
1. défendre	__________	__________
2. capitaine	__________	__________
3. pardonner	__________	__________
4. bouton	__________	__________
5. grammaire	__________	__________
6. moutarde	__________	__________

Answers to Middle English Exercises

1. Spelling

1. daughter	4. nephew
2. to find	5. to keep
3. to learn	6. heart

2. Words Used by Chaucer

1. battles	5. fought
2. begin	6. instead
3. beside	7. season
4. could	8. time

3. Loanwords from French

1. active	4. subject
2. music	5. judgement (judgment)
3. paper	6. person

4. Vocabulary

1. defend	(verb suffix *-re* dropped)
2. captain	(second syllable *-i-* dropped)
3. pardon	(verb suffix *-er* dropped)
4. button	(vowel changes to /u/, doubled medial consonant added)
5. grammar	(second syllable shortened to *-mar*, unstressed)
6. mustard	(vowel changes to /u/, letter *s* added)

Remind your students that the stress usually shifts away from the final syllable when a French word is Anglicized, and that vowel sounds also differ in many cases.

Early Modern English (c. 1500 – 1800)

Expansion of Vocabulary (1500–1650)

The English Language Comes into Its Own

The transition from Middle English to Modern English began in the sixteenth century when several factors came together to produce a period of extraordinary vitality and progress in the development of the language. During this period—the Renaissance—a great revival of interest in learning swept over England and much of Europe, leading people to become more aware of the importance of language as they studied the writings of the past. Furthermore, many words from other languages (especially Latin and Greek) were introduced into English as a result of this growing interest in the writings of antiquity. We have already seen that the growing availability of printed books made more and more people aware of the need for clarity and consistency in spelling and usage.

Until the sixteenth century, French continued to be the prestigious literary language, and Latin remained the international language for serious scholarly work well into the seventeenth century. However, the influence of other languages gradually diminished as the English language continued to develop. A sense of literary nationalism swept over England as an increasingly large reading public came to realize that English could assume its place among the major languages of the world.

The work of the poet John Skelton (1460-1529) shows how important the English language had become and how rapidly its vocabulary was expanding in the sixteenth century. Skelton is credited with introducing about 1500 new words into the English language, many of them derived from his study of Latin. A few of the many new words contributed by Skelton are these:

accumulate (L *accumulare*)

attempt (L *attemptare*)

celebrate (L *celebrare*)

concern (L *concernere*)

describe (L *describere*)

economy (Gk *oikonomia*)

gravity (L *gravis,* heavy)

imitation (L *imitatus* from *imitari,* to copy)

lucky (ME *lucke,* from Middle High German *gelücke*)

miserable (L *miserabilis*)

seriousness (Fr *serieux* [from L *serius*] +OE suffix *-nes*)

steadily (OE *stede,* place)

variety (L *varietas*)

These words illustrate principles of Anglicization that are found throughout the history of the language, especially the change or elimination of Latin verb suffixes and the mixture of German and Latin elements (as in *seriousness*).

The Search for Spelling Conventions: *Mulcaster's* Elementarie

The hybrid nature of the English language has been the source of many questions about the spelling of words, not only those retained from Old English but also those taken over from other languages. Our alphabet of 26 letters must represent at least 44 different sounds, or *phonemes.* If we are puzzled today by some of the varied spellings of the same sound and by the use of the same letter or letters to represent different sounds, then the writer and reader of the sixteenth century must have been even more mystified.

A giant step toward standard spelling and usage was taken in 1582 with the publication of Richard Mulcaster's *Elementarie*, one of the earliest attempts to deal with the English language as it was actually spoken and written. Some of the spelling principles established by Mulcaster are these:

1. Remove all unnecessary letters. In earlier days, simple words with short vowels were spelled with extra consonants at the end (*tubb*, *bedd*). Mulcaster established the Consonant-Vowel-Consonant (CVC) pattern as the norm for spelling words or syllables with short vowels (*tub*, *bed*).

2. Include letters that are needed to indicate correct pronunciation (the *t* in *catch*, for example).

3. Use a final silent *e* to mark long vowels and to distinguish them from short vowels (e.g., *hop* for the short vowel and *hope* for the long vowel). Mulcaster called this the *qualifying E*: "I call that E, qualifying, whose absence or presence, somtime altereth the vowell, somtime the consonant going next before it" (Campagnac, 1925, p. 123).

Mulcaster established other spelling principles as well, but these three are particularly significant. The third item helped to establish a guideline that eventually brought order to the varied and chaotic spelling of short and long vowels that made sixteenth-century English confusing.

Instability in Early Modern English

Although one of Mulcaster's goals was to bring order to English spelling, several features of his use of the language appear archaic to us today. Some of the unusual spellings of his time resulted when printers varied the spelling of words in order to make lines of print come out the right length in different locations. One common practice in the early sixteenth century was the use of *mo* and *moe* to mean "more in number" with plural nouns whose individual elements could be counted, such as *mo horses* or *mo cattle*. The word *more* was at first used to mean "greater in quantity" with singular, abstract nouns that did not contain individual quantifiable elements, as in *more art* or *more honesty* (Barber, 1976, p. 230).

The word *and* was often represented by the ampersand (&), and the *tilde* (~) was placed over a letter to indicate that the following letter was not written out but could be inferred from context. This sign was often used to represent the letters *m* or *n*, as in *frõ* for *from* and *cã* for *can*. Mulcaster always had all the letters written out in words such as *number* and *then* when listing proper spellings in tabular form, but printers often set these words with the *tilde* in place of *m* and *n* in the text itself.

Although Mulcaster did establish the final silent *e* as a marker for long-vowel words (*face, hope, mine*), other vowel spellings remained less clear. Words that we now spell with vowel digraphs (*need, soap, see*) were either spelled with final *e* (*nede, sope*) or had no marker of any sort (*se* for *see*). Some other words could be spelled several different ways: *childeren, childern,* or *children*, for example. Mulcaster also included the following words in his list of proper spellings:

bycause (because)	quik (quick)
duble (double)	som (some)
hir (her)	theie (they)
pece (piece)	throte (throat)
peple (people)	tung (tongue)

These few examples show that many of the conventions we use today were still far from settled in Mulcaster's time.

Language in Shakespeare's Day: The Great Vowel Shift

During the lifetime of William Shakespeare (1564-1616), most of the simplification of Old English inflections and the other grammatical changes of Middle English had already been accomplished. Changes in pronunciation continued, however, and the earlier practice of articulating all consonants had all but disappeared by the beginning of the seventeenth century. Pronunciation of vowels in Old English words had already begun to change by the fifteenth century: for example, the final vowel in *nama* (name) had diminished to the *schwa* sound before disappearing entirely. Even greater changes in the pronunciation of long vowels occurred during the period of Early Modern English and continued through the eighteenth century. These changes, taken as a whole, were so extensive and important in the development of the language that they have been called the **Great Vowel Shift**.

Some idea of the extent of this vowel shift is suggested by the following description of how the words *house, wife, he, her, wine,* and *moon* were pronounced in the fourteenth century:

> Chaucer lived in what would have sounded like a *hoos*, with his *weef*, and *hay* would romance *heer* with a bottle of *weena*, drunk by the light of the *moan*. In the two hundred years, from 1400 to 1600, which separated Chaucer and Shakespeare, the sounds of English underwent a substantial change to form the basis of Modern English pronunciation. (Yule, 1985, p. 174)

Some of these changes in long-vowel sounds were well established by the time of Shakespeare. For example, in Chaucer's day the word *beet* would have been pronounced *bait*, and the word *boat* would have been pronounced *boot*; by the seventeenth century, both words had assumed their present-day pronunciation. Other words changed pronunciation from Middle to Early Modern English, and then changed again into present-day English. As Yule pointed out, the word *house* (spelled *hūs* in Old English) would still have rhymed with *goose* in Chaucer's day, but by the sixteenth century it had changed first to *hose* (rhyming with *dose*) before changing again to its present pronunciation. We have given examples of only some of the vowel sounds that changed during the period from 1400 to 1800, but even these few show how important and extensive these changes were.

Orthography and Printing in Shakespeare's Day

The written language of Shakespeare's day retained a number of archaic features of *orthography*—the writing of words with proper letters following the accepted standards of the time. For example, the letters *u* and *v* still represented either the vowel or consonant, a practice that was not arbitrary even though it might appear so to us. Barber explains that "for the first letter of a word, the printer invariably selects *v*, and in other positions he invariably selects *u*" (1976, p. 15). This practice was normally followed by printers in Shakespeare's day but was not used so consistently in manuscripts.

Other features of earlier orthography included use of the long *s* (ſ), which looks like an *f* without the cross-bar. This form was used to represent the letter *s* at every point in a word except as an initial capital or as the final letter. Also, the letter *i* continued to serve for both the vowel *i* and the consonant *j*, as it had done for centuries. The elongated *i*, which was to become the letter *j*, had not been adopted consistently at this time. English printing of this period can be seen in the following passage taken from the first folio edition (1623) of Shakespeare's plays. These are the famous lines spoken by Marc Antony in Act III of *Julius Caesar:*

> *An.*Friends,Romans,Countrymen,lend me your ears:
> I come to bury *Cæſar*,not to praiſe him :
> The euill that men do, liues after them,
> The good is oft enterred with their bones,
> So let it be with *Cæſar.* The Noble *Brutus;*
> Hath told you *Cæſar* was Ambitious :
> If it were ſo, it was a greeuous Fault,
> And greeuouſly hath *Cæſar* anſwer'd it.
> Heere, vnder leaue of *Brutus*,and the reſt
> (For *Brutus* is an Honourable man,
> So are they all; all Honourable men)
> Come I to ſpeake in *Cæſars* Funerall.

Shakespeare, *Julius Caesar*, Act III (Hinman, 1968, p. 729)

To a great extent our concept of earlier forms of written English has been influenced by the practices of printers in centuries past. For example, Caxton and others used the Middle English spelling of words as they existed when they began their work in the late fifteenth century. However, as pronunciation continued to change throughout Early Modern English, the spelling of many words ultimately did not accurately reflect their sound. This is obvious in words such as *knee* and *write*, whose OE spellings *cnēow* and *wrītan* contained letters that were originally sounded and that were retained in their written forms long after the practice of articulating all consonants had been abandoned. This contrast between sound and symbol became even greater when printers from countries such as Holland and Belgium set out to print books in English, bringing their own concepts of sound-symbol relationships to a language that was not their own.

Shakespeare's efforts were devoted to writing plays in language that suited the requirements of comedy, history, and tragedy—his concern was with the *performance* of his plays, not with their publication.

> And since Shakespeare evidently paid little heed to the printing of his plays, the printing house was more than a little involved in establishing texts of Shakespeare's works. If we assume that what we call Shakespearean was indeed by Shakespeare, then many of the puzzling aspects of the text, such as the varying styles of punctuation, can be solved only by a study of printing-house conditions, an identification of the compositors, and a reconstruction of the history of the transmission of the text—and for each work individually. (Spevack, 1985, pp. 343-44)

Spelling Conventions

Our concepts of spelling and usage have been influenced to a great extent by printers who first published the literary works and other documents that make up our heritage of the English language. We sometimes find that one or another of our present-day spelling conventions exists for no better reason than that some Norman scribe or Belgian printer first spelled an English word in his own way, based in large part on the sound-spelling principles of his native language, and the word has been spelled that way ever since. For example, the spellings of the OE word *gāst* (from the Old High German *geist*, meaning "spirit") and the ME *gost* clearly indicated the pronunciation in their respective periods. However, by the late sixteenth century the additional letter *h* began to appear in books printed by Dutch and Belgian printers (in fact, the word is spelled *gheest* in Flemish), and the spelling *ghost* has persisted since that time.

From the sixteenth century into the eighteenth, the spelling conventions for many words was determined by referring to their original forms as a guide. We have already seen that Old English words such as *sweord* and *cniht* contained consonant letters that were spoken in the tenth century but are no longer sounded in the modern spellings *sword* and *knight*. When consistent spelling patterns were imposed on words that had changed so drastically in pronunciation, the results sometimes represented an unusual mixture of old and modern practices.

This is especially true of the words *should, would,* and *could,* which obviously share a common graphemic base in their modern spellings even though the written pattern does not exactly match the sound. The Old English words *sceolde* (which became *sholde* in ME) and *wolde* (unchanged in ME) eventually assumed their current spellings *should* and *would*. In these cases it is possible to see that the letter *l* is a vestige of their original spelling *and* sound, even though the *l* became silent in Modern English. However, the OE word *cuthe* (later spelled *couthe* or *coude* in ME) never did contain an *l*, even though its modern spelling is *could*. At some point the decision was made to establish a consistent spelling pattern for these three related words even though the retention of the letter *l* was valid for only two of them.

The same rationale applies to words adapted from Latin. Frequently an effort was made to establish spelling conventions in English that mirrored some features of the original words even though pronunciation no longer matched written symbols. This can be seen in a word such as *debt,* which was spelled *dette* both in Old French and in Middle English. During the period of fascination with Latin words in the sixteenth and seventeenth centuries, the spelling was changed to *debt* to reflect the original Latin *debitum,* a form of the verb *debēre* meaning "to owe." The same thing happened with the verb *to doubt,* spelled *douten* in ME and *douter* in Old French. The letter *b* was added to reflect the Latin source *dubitare,* "to doubt, be uncertain."

We can now see the source of the conflict that has arisen over the centuries as people tried to establish standard English spellings that also reflected the original spelling and meaning of words from other languages. A knowledge of the etymology of words can certainly be helpful, and clues to this etymology often are imbedded in modern spellings. On the other hand, language reformers have advocated spellings such as *det* and *dout* that would establish a clear match between sound and symbol.

Some of the spellings we now use, complete with "silent letters" and other anomalies, were established in the first printed books and have remained the norm ever since, largely because it would have been all but impossible to change printed texts after they were published. Other spellings were established in the period of Early Modern English, when a concern for the derivation of words from Latin and Greek led to spellings such as those found in *debt* and *doubt*. Even though the spelling conventions of some words do require us to include letters that are not pronounced, a knowledge of why and how these spellings developed allows us to see that there is a reason for their seeming irregularities. In some cases, these spellings even give us clues to the original meaning of the words and can thus help us to understand their meaning more clearly.

The Need for an English Dictionary

Today we can easily turn to a dictionary to check the spelling or definition of any word, but at the beginning of the seventeenth century there was no true dictionary of the English language to provide writers with a guide to standard usage and spelling. Shakespeare did use Thomas Wilson's *Art of Rhetorique* (1553), a well-known text that advocated clear, direct writing and opposed the use of obscure words contrived from Latin elements. Other than this and Mulcaster's *Elementarie*, very little help was available to writers in the early period of Modern English.

> Langland, Chaucer, and Malory at best had access to lists of "hard words" in certain subjects, usually glossed by Latin words which they were assumed to have learnt at school or university. Spenser and some other Renaissance writers appended explanations to some of their works so that readers would understand the more difficult words.... The early plays of Shakespeare were written before the first English dictionary was published. It is self-evident therefore that English literature can proceed at the highest level of performance without the existence of elaborate lexicons and grammars. The spoken language has always proceeded without recourse to dictionaries. (Burchfield, 1985, pp. 77-78)

The earliest dictionaries in the seventeenth century were intended to define only difficult and unusual words, not every word in the language. One of the first books of this type was *A Table Alphabeticall*, published in 1604 by Robert Cawdrey. The purpose of this volume was to teach "the true writing, and vnderstanding of hard vsuall English wordes, borrowed from the Hebrew, Greeke, Latine, or French. &c." This was one of the first publications that could be considered a dictionary of any sort. It contained about 2,500 hard words "with the interpretation thereof—by plaine English words, gathered for the benefit & helpe of Ladies, Gentlewomen, or any other unskilfull persons."

The first book to call itself an English dictionary was a two-part work by Henry Cockeram, published in London in 1623 and entitled *The English Dictionarie: or, an Interpreter of hard English Words*. It claimed that it would not only help readers understand the more difficult authors but also lead to "speedy attaining of an elegant perfection of the English tongue, both in reading, speaking, and writing."

The first part of Cockeram's dictionary contained brief definitions of words that may have been important to the seventeenth-century lady or gentleman who wanted to impress polite society with a display of erudition. Some of Cockeram's words are of the "inkhorn" variety, obscure contrivances cobbled together from bits and pieces of Latin. For example, the Latin prefix *ab-* (away from), when combined with the Latin word *equus* (horse), yields the verb *abequitate*: to ride away on horseback. Not all entries are quite so humorously inventive, but in some cases the definition is as obscure as the word itself:

Acersecomicke. One whose haire was never cut.

Acyrologicall. An unproper speech.

Adecasticke. One that will doe just howsoever.

The second part of Cockeram's dictionary reversed the process, listing everyday words and following them with more arcane terms meaning approximately the same thing. This was intended to show people how the words in the first part could be used to turn simple, direct statements into obscure, complicated ones that would presumably be more impressive. For example, the adjective *doubtful* could be replaced by *amphibologicall*, and "to breath [*sic*] or blow on" something was to *adhalate*. Fortunately this fascination with more extreme inkhorn terms eventually ran its course.

The Search for Standards of Usage (1650–1800)

Lack of Guidelines

The sixteenth century—the age of Elizabethan English— was a period of rapid growth in vocabulary and of great instability in conventions of spelling and usage. Spelling in particular was largely phonetic and often reflected regional dialects. It is not uncommon to find the same word spelled several different ways on a single page, simply because the writer had no way to determine what the correct spelling should be.

These problems persisted into the seventeenth century. In 1679 the poet and playwright John Dryden wrote of the difficulties inherent in the spelling and grammar of English. He pointed out that the French had established an academy in 1634 to develop a proper grammar and dictionary for their language, and he hoped the same thing could be done for English:

> And as our *English* is a composition of the dead and living Tongues, there is requir'd a perfect knowledge, not onely of the *Greek* and *Latine*, but of the Old *German*, the *French* and the *Italian*: and to help all these, a conversation with those Authours of our own, who have written with the fewest faults in prose and verse. But how barbarously we yet write and speak, your Lordship knows, and I am sufficiently sensible in my own *English*. For I am often put to a stand, in considering whether what I write be the Idiom of the Tongue, or false Grammar, and nonsence couch'd beneath that specious Name of *Anglicisme*; and have no other way to clear my doubts, but by translating my *English* into *Latine*, and thereby trying what sence the words will bear in a more stable language. (Roper, 1984, p. 222)

We may find it remarkable that a seventeenth-century English writer felt the need to translate his work into Latin in order to make sure it made sense in terms of a more stable language that had clear rules of grammar. Even into the eighteenth century, Latin continued to exert a strong influence on the grammar as well as the lexicon of English, and attempts to establish standards of English usage were based on Latin as the model. The mixture of German, French, Latin, and Greek words was still difficult to deal with, and turning all this into proper English continued to cause problems more than a thousand years after the Anglo-Saxons had brought *Englisc* to Britain.

Samuel Johnson's Dictionary

Although seventeenth-century dictionaries were restricted to a small number of "hard" words, a different approach was taken by Nathaniel Bailey in his *Universal Etymological Dictionary of the English Language* of 1721. This pioneering work was "the first to pay attention to current usage, the first to feature etymology, the first to syllabify, the first to give illustrative quotations, the first to include illustrations, and the first to indicate pronunciation" (Guralnik, 1951, p. 124). Bailey's work also formed the basis for an even more influential dictionary which appeared in 1755.

This was *A Dictionary of the English Language* by Samuel Johnson (1709-1784), who built on and extended Bailey's work. On the title page Johnson states that "The WORDS are deduced from their ORIGINALS, and ILLUSTRATED in their DIFFER-ENT SIGNIFICATIONS by EXAMPLES from the best WRIT-ERS." Because everyday speech was "copious without order, and energetick without rules" (as he said in his preface), Johnson selected these "examples from the best writers" to show correct usage of the words in his dictionary. Although at first he hoped to establish a standard that would not change, he later acknowl-edged that no lexicographer could compile a dictionary that would "embalm his language, and secure it from corruption and decay."

Johnson went to great lengths to show that many words varied in meaning depending on context: "He has been equaled but never surpassed in the particularly nerve-straining exercise of tearing a word down into all the senses in which it is used" (Guralnik, 1951, p. 125). A few of the sixty-eight entries for the verb *to run* are given on page 61.

Despite its limitations, this dictionary set the standard for the language well into the following century. It also fixed many of the spellings which still trouble us today because they reflect Johnson's limited knowledge of etymology and his lack of con-cern for the problems caused by different spellings for the same sound. While Johnson was codifying the spelling and meaning of words, others were establishing guidelines for grammar.

To RUN. *v. n.* pret. *ran.* [*rinnan*, Gothick ; ẏnnan, Saxon ; *rennen*, Dutch.]

1. To move fwiftly ; to ply the legs in fuch a manner, as that both feet are at every ftep off the ground at the fame time ; to make hafte ; to pafs with very quick pace.

   Their feet *run* to evil, and make hafte to fhed blood. *Prov.*

   Laban *ran* out unto the man unto the well. *Gen.* xxiv. 29.

   When fhe knew Peter's voice, fhe *ran* in, and told how Peter ftood before the gate.   *Acts* xii. 14.

   Since death's near, and *runs* with fo much force,
   We muft meet firft, and intercept his courfe.   *Dryden.*

   He *ran* up the ridges of the rocks amain.   *Dryden.*

   Let a fhoe-boy clean your fhoes and *run* of errands. *Swift.*

2. To ufe the legs in motion.

   Seldom there is need of this, till young children can *run* about.   *Locke.*

3. To move in a hurry.

   The prieft and people *run* about,
   And at the ports all thronging out,
   As if their fafety were to quit
   Their mother.   *Benj. Johnfon.*

4. To pafs on the furface, not through the air.

   The Lord fent thunder, and the fire *ran* along upon the ground.   *Exodus* ix. 25.

5. To rufh violently.

   Let not thy voice be heard, left angry fellows *run* upon thee, and thou lofe thy life.   *Judges* xviii. 25.

   Now by the winds and raging waves I fwear,
   Your fafety more than mine was thus my care ;
   Left of the guide bereft, the rudder loft,
   Your fhip fhou'd *run* againft the rocky coaft.   *Dryden.*

   They have avoided that rock, but *run* upon another no lefs dangerous.   *Burnet's Theory of the Earth.*

   I difcover thofe fhoals of life which are concealed in order to keep the unwary from *running* upon them.   *Addifon.*

6. To take a courfe at fea.

   Running under the ifland Clauda, we had much work to come by the boat.   *Acts* xxvii. 16.

7. To contend in a race.

   A horfe-boy, being lighter than you, may be trufted to *run* races with lefs damage to the horfes.   *Swift.*

8. To fly ; not to ftand. It is often followed by *away* in this fenfe.

   My confcience will ferve me to *run* from this Jew, my mafter.   *Shakefp. Merchant of Venice.*

First eight entries for the verb *to run* from Samuel Johnson's *Dictionary of the English Language* (1755).

Authoritarian English

The years from 1650 to 1800 have been described as the period of "Authoritarian English" (Nist, 1966, p. 269 ff.). This label well suits the "age of reason" during which people tried to make sense of the dynamic development that the language had undergone in the years from 1500 to 1650. The period was characterized especially by a strong sense of the value of order and regulation.

> Adventurous individualism and the spirit of independence characteristic of the previous era give way to a desire for system and regularity. This involves conformity to a standard that the consensus recognizes as good. It sets up correctness as an ideal and attempts to formulate rules or principles by which correctness may be defined and achieved. (Baugh and Cable, 1978, p. 253)

Perhaps the earliest attempt to establish a guide to English grammar was William Bullokar's *Bref Grammar*, published in 1586. Over the next century and a half a number of other grammars appeared, all with little effect on the development of the language. By the middle of the eighteenth century, however, the demand for clear answers to questions of correctness had become more emphatic than ever before.

In 1762 a *Short Introduction to English Grammar with Critical Notes* was published anonymously in London. The same book was published in Philadelphia in 1775, but this time the title page carried the name of the author: Robert Lowth (1710-1787), a professor of Hebrew at Oxford University who later became Bishop of London. It was Lowth's authoritarian attitude and insistence on absolute rules of grammar that set the tone for the final phase of the search for standards of usage. It was also this attitude that led some of his followers to exaggerate the importance of regularity for its own sake, leading to the kind of pedantry that ultimately stifles the spontaneous, inventive use of language.

> During the Renaissance period and later, the feeling grew that English grammar should be described in the terminology of Latin grammar. Sometimes that procedure was not objectionable, for many elements of the two languages were similar. But when the grammarians insisted upon finding in English

everything that existed in Latin, when they made of Latin a procrustean bed into which English must be in some way fitted, and when they ignored the fact that English was basically a Teutonic and not an Italic language, they did irreparable harm to many generations of persons who wanted to acquire a clear understanding of the structure and peculiarities of the language. (Hook and Mathews, 1956, pp. 31-32)

In spite of the many admirable features of the English language, Lowth found that it was sadly deficient in one important way: "Whatever other improvements it may have received, it hath made no advances in grammatical accuracy" (1775, p. iii). He lamented the lack of study of grammar in schools and hoped that his "notes" (as he called his comments on grammar) would show the need for this study. He also wasted no time in establishing his intention to right the wrongs of the past and prevent them in the future:

It will evidently appear from these notes, that our best authors have committed gross mistakes, for want of a due knowledge of English grammar, or at least of a proper attention to the rules of it. The examples there given are such as occurred in reading, without any very curious or methodical examination: and they might easily have been much increased in number by any one, who had leisure or phlegm enough to go through a regular course of reading with this particular view. (Lowth, 1775, p. viii)

No matter how great their renown, no authors of the past could provide a reliable guide for a grammarian such as Lowth.

For a really satisfactory standard he has to look higher—not at the actual sentences the authors wrote, but at the sentences they would have written if they had understood grammar better, and practiced it more carefully—if they had, in fact, studied and followed the book he is in the process of composing. To a non-grammarian this reasoning may seem a little peculiar, but neither Lowth nor his followers seem to have been bothered by it. (Myers, 1966, p. 226)

We could too easily dismiss such views as mere pedantry, but there were valuable features in Lowth's grammar and there is no question that the language had reached a stage that demanded some attempt to establish guidelines for proper usage. Lowth proposed some new "rules" and perpetuated others: for example, the distinction between *shall* and *will*, the correct use of the pronouns *who* and *whom*, the difference between *lie* and *lay*, and the idea that words with absolute meaning could not be used in comparative or superlative degrees. (One straight line cannot be "straighter" than another, and one circle cannot be the "roundest" of the group: a line is either *straight* or it isn't, and a circle is by definition *round* or it is not a circle.)

Lowth's ideas certainly had their limitations, but his analysis of grammatical structure was more usable than others had been, and his work found ready acceptance in the schools. "Many of the constructions he criticized were in fact awkward or ambiguous; and most of the rules he laid down are reasonably sensible if not pushed too far" (Myers, 1966, p. 228).

Conclusion

We can see that by 1800 standard practices had been fairly well established for the spelling and grammar of English. Although the language has continued to develop since that time and new words have been added in science and communications in particular, the basic structure of English has not undergone the drastic changes or periods of instability we encountered in the earlier stages of English. Because it is so resilient and its underlying structure is so strong, the English language has been able to absorb words from many other languages and adapt them to principles of grammar and usage that have prevailed for more than two centuries.

Early Modern English: Exercises

1. Spelling

Look at these words taken from sixteenth-century literature; then write their modern spellings.

1. allredie ______________________________

2. bene ______________________________

3. birdes ______________________________

4. continew ______________________________

5. her selfe ______________________________

6. powre ______________________________

7. starre ______________________________

8. suddain ______________________________

9. theyre ______________________________

Early Modern English: Exercises

2. Elizabethan English

Look at the sentences below, written with spellings found in the language of the late sixteenth and early seventeenth centuries, the age of Queen Elizabeth I (1533-1603); then rewrite the sentences with modern spellings.

1. The clowds will soone passe and the sunne will be shyning.

____

____ .

2. The Queene her selfe doth loue musicke.

____ .

3. This knight hath suffred deepe woundes in battel.

____ .

4. "They cannot finde that path, which first was showne,
    But wander too and fro in waies unknowne,..."

____

____

____

____

Early Modern English: Exercises

3. Synonyms

This exercise deals with synonyms that originated in different languages. Look at each English word in the first column and then indicate by letter the word in the second column derived from French or Latin that means much the same thing.

English	**French or Latin**
1. folk _____	A. action
2. help _____	B. cottage
3. strength _____	C. people (F *peuple*; L *populus*)
4. hut _____	D. demand (F *demander*; L *demandare*)
5. deed _____	E. aid (F *aider*; L *adjuvare*)
6. ask _____	F. fortitude (L *fortitudo*)

Early Modern English: Exercises

4. Latin Loanwords

Many Latin words had entered the English language by the seventeenth century, sometimes directly, sometimes by way of French. Look at each definition and at the Latin elements that make up the English word defined. Then write the modern spelling for each English word derived from these Latin (L) elements.

1. **Definition**: "To be made up of or composed of"

   from L *com-, con-* (with) + *sistere* (to take a stand)

   Modern English Word: _______________________________

2. **Definition**: "To investigate or study; to travel for discovery"

   from L *ex-* (out of, from) + *plorare* (to cry out)

   Modern English Word: _______________________________

3. **Definition**: "To express grief or discontent"

   from L *com-* (with) + *plangere* (to lament)

   Modern English Word: _______________________________

4. **Definition**: "Lack of sufficent regard or esteem"

   from L *dis-* (apart, not, opposite of) + *respicere* (to look back, regard)

   Modern English Word: _______________________________

Answers to Early Modern English Exercises

1. Spelling

1. already
2. been
3. birds
4. continue
5. herself

6. power
7. star
8. sudden
9. their

2. Elizabethan English

1. The clouds will soon pass and the sun will be shining.

2. The Queen herself does love music (or just "loves music").

3. This knight has suffered deep wounds in battle.

4. "They cannot find that path, which first was shown,
   But wander to and fro in ways unknown, . . ."
   (From Edmund Spenser's *The Faerie Queene*,
   pub. 1590-96)

3. Synonyms

1. C
2. E
3. F

4. B
5. A
6. D

4. Latin Loanwords

1. consist
2. explore
3. complain
4. disrespect

Chapter V

American English

The English Language Comes to America

The First Colonists

At about the same time that the first folio edition of Shakespeare's work was being published, English settlers were establishing the first colonies in America. One of these early colonies was founded at Plymouth, Massachusetts, in 1620; a record of the settlers' experiences was kept by William Bradford, who became governor of the colony in 1621.

Bradford's chronicle, entitled *Of Plimoth Plantation*, shows how English was used by these first colonists in early seventeenth-century America. The beginning is given below in Bradford's own hand, followed by a printed transcription.

And first of ye occasion and indusments ther unto; the which that I may truly unfould, I must begine at ye very roote & rise of ye same. The which I shall endevor to manefest in a plaine stile; with singuler regard unto ye simple trueth in all things, at least as near as my slender judgmente can attaine the same. (*Bradford's History "Of Plimoth Plantation,"* p. 3)

Aside from spellings such as *unfould* and *stile*, the passage is intelligible even though its meaning may not be entirely clear. The most obvious archaic feature is the word *ye*, which had evolved when printers sought a substitute for the *thorn* after it fell into disuse. The letter *y* was used as an abbreviated form of the letters *th* (just as the *thorn* had been used earlier), so the word *ye* is actually pronounced *the* in spite of its appearance.

The next excerpt gives Bradford's description of the first attempt by Myles Standish and a group of men to go ashore in November of 1620. At first they discovered a cleared area where Indians had planted corn:

> And proceeding furder they saw new-stuble wher corne had been set ye same year, also they found wher latly a house had been, wher some planks and a great ketle was remaining, and heaps of sand newly padled with their hands, which they, digging up, found in them diverce faire Indean baskets filled with corne, and some in eares, faire and good, of diverce collours, which seemed to them a very goodly sight, (haveing never seen any shuch before). (*Bradford's History "Of Plimoth Plantation,"* p. 99)

Students can look at this passage and identify those spelling conventions that differ today from those of Bradford's time. For example, we use a doubled consonant to indicate short vowels in stressed syllables (as contrasted with *ketle* and *padle*) and we drop the final *e* before adding *-ing* in words such as *having*. We can also see some spellings that have now taken forms different from those of the seventeenth century: *further* rather than *furder* and *such* rather than *shuch*, for example. Some words in present-day American English are also different from their British spellings, as in the use of *s* rather than *c* in words such as *diverse*.

American English before the Revolution

The use of the English language in the mid-eighteenth century can be seen in the writing of George Washington. The example below is taken from the journal he kept while surveying land in Maryland in 1748. Washington described an encounter with Indians and gave an amusing account of their manner of dancing, or *dauncing* as it was spelled and pronounced in his day:

> They clear a Large Circle & make a great Fire in ye middle. Men seats themselves around it. Ye speaker makes a grand

speech, telling them in what manner they are to daunce. After
he has finishd ye best Dauncer jumps up as one awaked out of
a sleep, & Runs & Jumps about ye Ring in a most comicle
manner. He is followed by ye Rest. Then begins there musicians to Play. Ye musick is a Pot half full of water, with a
Deerskin streched over it as tight as it can, & a goard with
some shott in it to rattle & a Piece of an horse's tail tied to it to
make it look fine. Ye one keeps rattling & ye others drumming
all ye while ye others is Dauncing. (Ford, 1889, p. 3)

As with the passages from Bradford's chronicle written more
than a century earlier, we find a number of spellings and other
features (such as the ubiquitous *ye*) that are very different from
those of present-day English. Notable differences are found in
words such as *finishd*, in which the past tense is formed by the
addition of the letter *d* alone, and *streched*, which omits the
letter *t* we use today. Other differences in grammar are obvious,
such as the constructions "men seats themselves" and "then
begins there musicians to play." Even by this time the difference
between *there* and *their* had not been clearly established.

Benjamin Franklin's "Idea of the English School"

Another example of American English of the Colonial period
can be found in the "Idea of the English School," written in 1751
by Benjamin Franklin (1706-1790). The passage given on the
next page provides a glimpse of Franklin's views on education
and gives us an example of the use of language in America at the
time when Samuel Johnson in England was completing his dictionary. The excerpt begins with Franklin's description of the
requirements for the first or lowest class in his proposed school.

We can see that the past tense is formed sometimes with *-'d*
(*sketch'd, receiv'd*) and sometimes with *-ed* (*expected, admitted*).
Any word ending with *t* or *d* would require the full *-ed* ending
because the inflection requires a new syllable after these letters
(*wait, waited*), while all other consonants could be followed by
-'d because the inflection would not require a separate syllable.
So far as orthography is concerned, the long *s* is still employed
everywhere except as the capital initial or the final letter and is
often joined to the next letter in words such as *first* and *most*.

Before Franklins' day, formal education had been largely
based on the concept of the classical school in which instruction

[1]

IDEA *of the* ENGLISH SCHOOL,

Sketch'd out for the Confideration of the TRU-STEES *of the* PHILADELPHIA ACADEMY.

IT is expected that every Scholar to be admitted into this School, be at leaft able to pronounce and divide the Syllables in Reading, and to write a legible Hand. None to be receiv'd that are under   Years of Age.

Firft or loweft CLASS.

LET the firft Clafs learn the *Englifh Grammar* Rules, and at the fame time let particular Care be taken to improve them in *Orthography*. Perhaps the latter is beft done by *Pairing* the Scholars, two of thofe neareft equal in their Spelling to be put together ; let thefe ftrive for Victory, each propounding Ten Words every Day to the other to be fpelt. He that fpells truly moft of the other's Words, is Victor for that Day ; he that is Victor moft Days in a Month, to obtain a Prize, a pretty neat Book of fome Kind ufeful in their future Studies. This Method fixes the Attention of Children extreamly to the Orthography of Words, and makes them good Spellers very early. 'Tis a Shame for a Man to be fo ignorant of this little Art, in his own Language, as to be perpetually confounding Words of like Sound and different Significations ; the Confcioufnefs of which Defect, makes fome Men, otherwife of good Learning and Underftanding, averfe to Writing even a common Letter.

A

LET

Benjamin Franklin's "Idea of the English School," 1751
(Miller, 1974, p. 283)

was given in Latin. Franklin advocated to the trustees of the Philadelphia Academy that there should be not only a traditional classical school for those going on to college but also a complete secondary school providing education for those who planned to pursue a trade or profession. The curriculum of Franklin's proposed "English School" would include history, geography, and literature as well as the traditional study of grammar and logic.

> The principal innovation, and a striking one, was that the instruction itself would be conducted not in Latin, but entirely in English. The use of the vernacular language was the crucial issue and the main departure from the traditional school in Franklin's proposal. English, the common tongue, would set the basis and the underlying tone of the new school. (Best, 1962, pp. 13-14)

This proposal reflects Franklin's concern for the purely utilitarian value of education as well as his lack of esteem for the more traditional type of education that focused on the writings of classical Greece and Rome. At the end of his "Idea of the English School," Franklin made clear the value of his practical plan of education:

> Thus instructed, Youth will come out of this School fitted for learning any Business, Calling or Profession, except such wherein Languages are required; and tho' unacquainted with any antient or foreign Tongue, they will be Masters of their own, which is of more immediate and general Use. (Best, 1962, p. 171)

Establishing an American Language

The Contributions of Noah Webster (1758-1843)

Following the Revolutionary War, Noah Webster (as Franklin had already done) rejected all things British and advocated both a more practical form of education and the establishment of a truly American language:

> As an independent nation, our honor requires us to have a system of our own, in language as well as government. Great Britain, whose children we are, and whose language we speak, should no longer be *our* standard; for the taste of her writers is

already corrupted, and her language on the decline. (Webster, 1789, p. 20)

This extreme view was not sustained very long even by Webster himself. The works of Burns and Wordsworth, for example, hardly represent a decline of language or a corruption of literary tastes. However, Webster's statement does show the fervor with which he approached the task of establishing a language worthy and representative of an independent nation.

As his contribution to this patriotic effort, Webster began the ambitious task of writing the first American elementary textbooks, three volumes to be known collectively as *A Grammatical Institute of the English Language*. The first volume, a speller, appeared in 1783, followed by a grammar in 1784 and a reader in 1785. The speller was reprinted in 1787 with the title *The American Spelling Book* and again in 1829 as *The Elementary Spelling Book*. Its distinctive binding earned it the name "Blue-Back Speller," and it was this edition that became extraordinarily popular and sold in great quantities.

Webster's "Blue-Back Speller"

Webster's Speller begins with a pronunciation key in which vowel sounds are assigned numbers that are used to identify the sounds throughout the book. For example, all long vowels are assigned to category 1 (*name, time, note*, etc.); all short vowels to category 2 (*hat, let, but*); the *broad a* (as Webster calls it) to category 3 (*tall, cost*); and so on through category ten, which contains the diphthongs in *joy* and *loud*.

Lessons are organized into tables of syllables or words designed to show how these vowels are to be pronounced when combined with consonants. Table I begins with vowels preceded or followed by single consonants (*ba, be, bi, bo, bu, by; eb, ib, ob*, etc.) and then combined with blends and digraphs (*ble, cle, ple, fle; chi, dri, fri, gli*, etc.). Table II introduces one-syllable words containing vowels from several categories, each indicated by the appropriate number over the list of words (Category 2: *bag, cag, gag, hag, brag, drag, flag*, etc.; Category 5: *clog, flog, frog, grog*; and so on). The beginning of Table III shows how these word lists were presented:

TABLE III

Lesson I.

Blank²	blush²	fleet¹	brace¹	price¹	brine¹
flank	flush	sheet	chase	slice	shine
frank	plush	street	grace	spice	swine
prank	crush	greet	space	twice	twine

Lesson II.

Band²	bless²	crime¹	broke¹	blade¹	blame¹
grand	dress	chime	choke	spade	flame
stand	press	prime	cloke	trade	shame
strand	stress	slime	smoke	shade	frame

Examples of (1) long-vowel and (2) short-vowel words from Webster's "Blue-Back Speller" (1831)

This pattern of organization continues with words of two syllables accented on the first (*ba ker, ci der, cra zy*), then accented on the second (*a bide, a like, be fore, con trol*, for example). (Webster usually leaves blank spaces between syllables to set them apart.) Words of three, and then four, syllables are grouped according to placement of the stressed syllable, followed by lists of words with unique sound-spelling features: the /k/ sound in *chorus*; "Words in which *h* is pronounced before *w*, though written after it" (as in *whale* and *wheeze*); and so on. The book ends with lists of cities, rivers, and mountains in America, all grouped by number of syllables and location of stress: Bar′ ne gat, Os′ si py; Che buc′ to, Po soom′ suc.

Word lists are interspersed with passages requiring students to apply their knowledge to reading itself, or at least to the sounding out of words arranged into sentences. Bible verses become pedagogically valid when they contain words fitting the syllable patterns under study, as in this example of "Words not exceeding three syllables, divided":

> THE wick-ed flee when no man pur-su-eth; but the right-e-ous are as bold as a li-on.

Many other passages sing the praises of virtue and warn against the evils of negative thinking:

> The cheerful man hears the lark in the morning, the pensive man hears the nightingale in the evening.
>
> He who desires no virtue in a companion, has no virtue himself; and that state is hastening to ruin, in which no difference is made between good and bad men.

The reason for the popularity of the Blue-Back Speller is that "the primary purpose of a spelling book in Webster's time was, and always had been, to teach children to read" (Monaghan, 1983, p. 31). As Franklin had emphasized in his "Idea of the English School," spelling was viewed as the foundation on which students would develop their ability to read and write. This "alphabet method" was the only decoding method known at the time; it formed the basis of language instruction well into the nineteenth century.

Webster's Spelling Reforms

Although he was at first opposed to any changes in spelling, Webster later became convinced that spelling should reflect pronunciation and that irregularities should be swept away to clear the path for a new American language:

> The question now occurs; ought the Americans to retain these faults which produce innumerable inconveniencies in the acquisition and use of the language, or ought they at once to reform these abuses, and introduce order and regularity into the orthography of the AMERICAN TONGUE? (Webster, 1789, pp. 393-94)

In order to "reform these abuses," Webster maintained that unnecessary letters should be removed and that various spellings of the same sound should be changed to fit a single standard. For example, *head* and *bread* should be spelled *hed* and *bred*; the various spellings for /ē/ in *mean*, *grief*, and *key* should fit a single pattern in *meen*, *greef*, and *kee*; and the *ch* in French words such as *machine* should change to *masheen* (Webster, 1789, pp. 394-95).

Webster cited a number of benefits that would result from these changes: learning the language would be much easier because orthography would be regular; pronunciation would be improved because sound-spelling patterns would be more consistent; and this reform would set American orthography apart from that of England, thereby encouraging the publication of books in America because the English would never accept a standard set anywhere else. This last was especially important to Webster, who stressed that "a *national language* is a band of *national union*" and urged that every effort be made "to render the people of this country *national*" (Webster, 1789, p. 397).

Franklin and Webster dismissed all objections to their proposed reforms as mere quibbles. They were sure that people already familiar with the "old" spellings would be able to master the new very quickly, and books written in the past could still be read because modifications would not be drastic. "In answer to the objection, that a change of orthography would obscure etymology, I would remark, that the etymology of most words is already lost, even to the learned, and to the unlearned, etymology is never known" (Webster, 1789, p. 400).

Webster's Dictionaries

The preceding statement may have represented Webster's view in 1789, but the extensive study required for the preparation of his dictionaries apparently changed his mind in later years. As he discovered that the origin of many words *could* be determined, he moved toward greater emphasis on etymology. However, "Webster's etymologies, for which he had taken ten years to study the world's languages, were sadly deficient, even for his own time" (Laundau, 1984, p. 546). Important progress in the study of linguistic change was being made in the early nineteenth century by philologists such as the German Jacob Grimm, but Webster was not familiar with this work before his dictionaries were published. Webster also based his pronunciations on those of his native New England: "The rest of the country was ignored or was considered to speak incorrectly" (Landau, 1984, p. 546).

Webster's *Compendious Dictionary of the English Language* (1806) was a one-volume work with very brief definitions designed for the busy, practical American. An excerpt shows how this dictionary was designed to provide short, simple definitions to readers who did not have time to bother with niceties of etymology or differing shades of meaning.

> Con'fcioufnefs, *n.* perception of what paffes in the
>   mind, attended with certainty
> Confcribed, *a.* formed round, circumfcribed
> Con'fcript, *a.* written, regiftered, enrolled
> Con'fcript, *n.* an enrolled militia man
> Confcrip'tion, *n.* an enrollment, a regiftering
> Con'fecrate, *v.t.* to dedicate, devote, hallow
> Con'fecrated, *pa.* dedicated, made facred
> Con'fecrater, *n.* one who confecrates or devotes
> Confecrátion, *n.* the act of making facred or holy
> Confectáneous, Confect'ary, *a.* following of courfe
> Confect'ary, *n.* a corollary, inference, deduction
> Confecútion, *n.* a train of confequences, fucceffion
> Confec'utive, *a.* following in order, fucceffive

Webster's *Compendious Dictionary* (1806)

Webster's two-volume *American Dictionary of the English Language* appeared in 1828 and was noticeably different from its predecessor in its more extensive treatment of words. As Webster made clear on his title page, this volume was concerned with genuine orthography and pronunciation and with accurate definition; however, it also dealt with "the origin, affinities and primary signification of English words, as far as they have been ascertained." The excerpt on the next page shows how thoroughly Webster treated these "origins and affinities" in his 1828 dictionary. For example, he traces the word *habit* back to its Latin source; softening the fiery rhetoric of his youth, Webster acknowledges "our mother tongue, the Anglo-Saxon" in discussing the letter *H*.

Although Webster did not succeed in having *hed* and *greef* and *masheen* accepted as valid spellings, he did make a number of other changes that continue to set American and British English apart. For example, he argued that the letter *u* in some British spellings (such as *labour*) was unnecessary and should be changed (to *labor*). Words such as *musick* and *publick* should be spelled *music* and *public*, especially because there was no need for the *k* in *musical* or *publicly*. The British suffix *-ence* in words such as *defence* should be changed to *-ense* because the original Latin word (*defensare*) contained an *s* and derived forms such as *defensive* were always written with *s*. The British ending *-re* in words such as *theatre* and *centre* was changed to *-er*. Verbs of two or more syllables ending with an unstressed

H.

H, is the eighth letter of the English Alphabet. It is properly the representative of the Chaldee, Syriac and Hebrew ה, which is the eighth letter in those alphabets. Its form is the same as the Greek H *eta*. It is not strictly a vowel, nor an articulation; but the mark of a stronger breathing, than that which precedes the utterance of any other letter. It is pronounced with an expiration of breath, which, preceding a vowel, is perceptible by the ear at a considerable distance. Thus, *harm* and *arm*, *hear* and *ear*, *heat* and *eat*, are distinguished at almost any distance at which the voice can be heard. H is a letter *sui generis*, but as useful in forming and distinguishing words as any other.

In our mother tongue, the Anglo-Saxon, and other Teutonic dialects, *h* sometimes represents the L. *c*, and the Gr. χ; as in *horn*, L. *cornu*, Gr. χερας; *hide*, G. *haut*, Sw. *hud*, D. *huid*, Dan. *hud*, L. *cutis*; Sax. *hlinian*, L. *clino*, Gr. χλινω, to lean; L. *celo*, to conceal, Sax. *helan*, G. *hehlen*, Dan. *hæler*. In Latin, *h* sometimes represents the Greek χ; as in *halo*, Gr. χαλαω; *hio, χαω*. In the modern European languages, it represents other guttural letters.

In English, *h* is sometimes mute, as in *honor*, *honest*; also when united with *g*, as in *right*, *fight*, *brought*. In *which*, *what*, *who*, *whom*, and some other words in which it follows *w*, it is pronounced before it, *hwich*, *hwat*, &c. As a numeral in Latin, H denotes 200, and with a dash over it H̄ 200,000.

As an abbreviation in Latin, H stands for *homo, hæres, hora*, &c.

HA, an exclamation, denoting surprise, joy or grief. With the first or long sound of *a*, it is used as a question, and is equivalent to "What do you say?" When repeated, *ha, ha*, it is an expression of laughter, or sometimes it is equivalent to "Well! it is so."

HAAK, *n.* A fish.   *Ainsworth.*

Habeas Corpus, [L. have the body.] A writ for delivering a person from false imprisonment, or for removing a person from one court to another, &c.   *Cowel.*

HAB'ERDASHER, *n.* [perhaps from G. *habe*, D. *have*, goods, and G. *tauschen*, to barter, to truck. If not, I can give no account of its origin.]

A seller of small wares; *a word little used or not at all in the U. States.*

HAB'ERDASHERY, *n.* The goods and wares sold by a haberdasher.

HAB'ERDINE, *n.* A dried salt cod.

   Ainsworth.

HAB'ERGEON, *n.* [Fr. *haubergeon*; Norm. *hauberiom*; Arm. *hobregon*. It has been written also *haberge, hauberk*, &c. G. *halsberge; hals*, the neck, and *bergen*, to save or defend.]

A coat of mail or armor to defend the neck and breast. It was formed of little iron rings united, and descended from the neck to the middle of the body.

   Encyc. Ex. xxviii.

HAB'ILE, *a.* Fit; proper. [*Not in use.*]

   Spenser.

HABIL'IMENT, *n.* [Fr. *habillement*, from *habiller*, to clothe, from L. *habeo*, to have.]

A garment; clothing; usually in the plural, *habiliments*, denoting garments, clothing or dress in general.

HABIL'ITATE, *v. t.* [Fr. *habiliter.*] To qualify. [*Not used.*]   *Bacon.*

HABILITA'TION, *n.* Qualification. [*Not in use.*]   *Bacon.*

HABILITY. [See *Ability.*]

HAB'IT, *n.* [Fr. *habit*; Sp. *habito*; It. *abito*; L. *habitus*, from *habeo*, to have, to hold. See *Have.*]

1. Garb; dress; clothes or garments in general.

 The scenes are old, the *habits* are the same,
 We wore last year.   *Dryden.*
 There are among the statues, several of Venus, in different *habits*.   *Addison.*

2. A coat worn by ladies over other garments.

3. State of any thing, implying some continuance or permanence; temperament or particular state of a body, formed by nature or induced by extraneous circumstances; as a costive or lax *habit* of body; a sanguine *habit*.

4. A disposition or condition of the mind or body acquired by custom or a frequent

syllable should not double the final consonant when inflected, as in *traveling* and *canceled* (Monaghan, 1983, pp. 120-21).

Conclusion

This survey of the development of English closes with Webster's *American Dictionary* of 1828. As we said in connection with British English, the language had by the nineteenth century reached a level of stability that has not been greatly altered in the past 200 years. Of course the language has changed and will continue to do so, but these changes have taken place within a structural framework that remains remarkably strong and resilient.

Some of the most notable developments since 1800 include the spread of English as the first or second language in many other countries throughout the world, the addition of words from more and more different languages, and the increasing number of words that describe the latest advances in science and technology.

This last category provides some of the most interesting manifestations of the adaptive powers of the English language. Over the past few years we have read of *astronauts* in *orbit*, of *telemetry* and *satellites* and *lunar* modules, and of *spacecraft* named *Apollo* and *Mercury*. All these words refer to the most recent developments in space exploration, but the words themselves originated long before flight was anything more than a dream:

Apollo: Greek and Roman god of sunlight, poetry, music

astro-: Greek *astēr* (star, heavens, outer space)

craft: OE *cræft* (strength; from Old High German *kraft*)

lunar: Latin *luna* (moon)

Mercury: Roman god of travel, commerce, and science; messenger of the other gods

metr-: Greek *metron* (measure)

module: Latin *modulus* (small measure; from *modus*, measure)

-naut: Greek *nautikos*, from *nautēs* (sailor), *naus* (ship)

orbit: Latin *orbis* (circle)

satellite: Latin *satelles* (attendant)

space: Latin *spatium* (area, interval of space or time)

tele-: Greek *tēle* (far off)

All these words originated more than 2,000 years ago in the languages of Greece and Rome, with one Germanic word for good measure. These ancient words have been adapted to the most recent technological innovations of the late twentieth century, and they are all held together in coherent sentences by the Anglo-Saxon workhorses *the, and, to, in,* and *of.* This union of Germanic function words with scientific terms derived from Greek and Latin stands as a perfect example of the strength and character of the English language as it has developed over the past fifteen centuries.

At the beginning of this historical survey we cited Ayers' observation that English should be studied in perspective amid the many tongues of humankind. Throughout this study we have also stressed the external influences that brought about many changes in the language over the centuries, and we have given examples of additions to the English lexicon from Old Norse, French, Latin, and Greek in particular. We close the circle by stressing the fact that the speech of the Anglo-Saxons was in fact a highly developed language in its own right, although one built on principles very different from those we use today. Students should not think that Old English was merely a quaint ancestor that was forced to yield to superior qualities of other languages. The opposite is the case. The underlying strength of the English language has enabled it to maintain a coherent framework as it absorbed influences from many sources over the centuries.

Pyles and Algeo point out that English, in spite of the many factors that have influenced it, has retained unique qualities rooted in its parent tongue. It has also allowed writers to create some of the most significant literature ever produced:

> It is not unlikely, in the light of writings by Englishmen in earlier times, that this would have been so even if we had never taken any words from outside the word hoard that has come down to us from those times. It is true that what we have borrowed has brought greater wealth to our word stock, but the true Englishness of our mother tongue has in no way been lessened by such loans, as those who speak and write it lovingly will always keep in mind. (Pyles and Algeo, 1982, p. 317)

Fittingly enough, the authors point out that this passage is composed exclusively of words found in the language of the Anglo-Saxons.

American English: Exercises

1. Spelling and Syntax in the Seventeenth Century

Read the following passage from William Bradford's *Of Plimoth Plantation* for the year 1623.

They haveing but one boat left and she not over well fitted, they were devided into severall companies, 6. or 7. to a gangg or company, and so wente out with a nett they had bought, to take bass & such like fish, by course, every company knowing their turne. No sooner was ye boate discharged of what she brought, but ye next company tooke her and wente out with her.

Write the modern spelling for each of these words:

1. gangg_______________   4. wente_______________

2. devided_______________   5. ye_______________

3. severall_______________   6. turne_______________

Now answer these questions:

1. How could the meaning of the first phrase "They haveing but one boat left" be written in modern terms?

2. How would we write "to take bass & such like fish" in modern terms?

3. What is the meaning of the passage "No sooner was ye boate discharged of what she brought"? How could it be made more clear to the modern reader, especially in relation to the rest of the sentence?

American English: Exercises

2. Spelling and Meaning in the Eighteenth Century

The following words are from *The Autobiography of Benjamin Franklin*, written between 1771 and 1789. Write the modern spellings for the first five words; then use a dictionary to find the meaning of the last five items, words that were important in Franklin's day but that are less often used today. (Make sure you find the meaning that applies to Franklin's day.)

1. extream _______________________________

2. enjoy'd _______________________________

3. thro' _______________________________

4. endeavour _______________________________

5. us'd _______________________________

6. ironmonger: _______________________________

7. journeyman: _______________________________

8. smith: _______________________________

9. mercantile: _______________________________

10. constable: _______________________________

American English: Exercises

Vocabulary in the Nineteenth Century

The following words are taken from Nathaniel Hawthorne's *The House of the Seven Gables* (1850). These words are seldom used in everyday speech today but were known to the literate reader of the nineteenth century. Use a collegiate or unabridged dictionary to find the meaning of each word and write that meaning in the space provided. In the parentheses indicate the language in which each word originated: Latin (L), Greek (Gk), or some other source (OE, ME, Fr).

1. epoch __________________________________ (   )

2. magnate ______________________________ (   )

3. edifice _______________________________ (   )

4. lattice _______________________________ (   )

5. venerable _____________________________ (   )

American English: Exercises

4. Etymology

Look at these Modern English words and then look at the words from other languages listed below them. After each Modern English word, indicate which of the other languages provided the elements used in that word. You need not write the complete words from the other languages; just indicate the sources (OE, Fr, L, Gk).

MODERN ENGLISH:

1. helicopter_____/_____   6. semicircle_____/_____

2. automobile_____/_____   7. speedometer_____/_____

3. outnumber_____/_____   8. television_____/_____

4. overabundant_____/_____   9. undernourished_____/_____

5. sandpaper_____/_____   10. microscope_____/_____

OLD ENGLISH (OE):

ofer (over)   *sant* (sand)   *spēd* (speed)

under (under; from Ger. *untar*)   *ūt* (out)

FRENCH (FR):

abondant (abundant)   *nourrir* (to nourish)

nombre (number)

LATIN (L):

circus (circle)   *semi* (half)   *videre, visus* (to see)

mobilis (from *movēre,* to move)

GREEK (GK):

heliko (spiral, helix)   *papyros* (paper)   *pteron* (wing)

tele (distant, far off)   *micro* (small)   *auto* (self, same)

skopos (from *skeptesthai,* to look at)   *metron* (measure)

Answers to American English Exercises

1. Spelling and Syntax in the Seventeenth Century

1. gang	2. divided	3. several
4. went	5. the	6. turn

1. Because they had only one boat left . . .
2. To take (catch) bass and other fish of that type . . .
3. As soon as one boat emptied its contents . . .

2. Spelling and Meaning in the Eighteenth Century

1. extreme	2. enjoyed	3. through
4. endeavor	5. used	

6. ironmonger: a dealer in iron and hardware.

7. journeyman: a worker who has learned a trade and works for another person, usually on a day-to-day basis.

8. smith: anyone who works in metals.

9. mercantile: relating to merchants or trading.

10. constable: a public officer responsible for keeping the peace.

3. Vocabulary in the Nineteenth Century

1. epoch: an instant of time or a period of time (Gk)

2. magnate: a person of rank or influence (L)

3. edifice: a large or massive structure (L)

4. lattice: a framework of crossed wood or metal strips (ME *latis*, Fr. *lattis*)

5. venerable: worthy of respect on account of age or attainment (L)

4. Etymology

1. Gk/Gk	2. Gk/L	3. OE/Fr	4. OE/Fr	5. OE/Gk
6. L/L	7. OE/Gk	8. Gk/L	9. OE/Fr	10. Gk/Gk

References

Alexander, Michael, trans. *The Earliest English Poems: A Bilingual Edition*. Berkeley: University of California Press, 1970.

Ayers, Donald M. *English Words from Latin and Greek Elements*. Tucson: University of Arizona Press, 1986.

Baker, Timothy. *The Normans*. London: Cassell, 1966.

Barber, Charles. *Early Modern English*. London: André Deutsch, 1976.

Baugh, Albert C., and Thomas Cable. *A History of the English Language,* 3rd ed. Englewood Cliffs, NJ: Prentice-Hall, 1978.

Best, John H., ed. *Benjamin Franklin on Education*. New York: Bureau of Publications, Teachers College, Columbia University, 1962.

Blake, Norman F. *Caxton's Own Prose*. London: André Deutsch, 1973.

__________. *The English Language in Medieval Literature*. London: J. M. Dent, 1977.

Bradford's History "Of Plimoth Plantation." From the original manuscript. With a report of the proceedings incident to the return of the manuscript to Massachusetts. Boston: Wright & Potter, 1901.

Burchfield, Robert. *The English Language*. Oxford and New York: Oxford University Press, 1985.

Campagnac, E. T., ed. *Mulcaster's Elementarie*. London: Oxford University Press, 1925.

Cawdrey, Robert. *A Table Alphabeticall of Hard Usual English Words*, 1604. A facsimile reproduction with an introduction by Robert A. Peters. Gainesville, FL: Scholars' Facsimiles and Reprints, 1966.

Caxton, William. *Sir Thomas Malory Le Morte d'Arthur printed by William Caxton 1485*. Reproduced in facsimile from the copy in the Pierpont Morgan Library, New York. London: The Scolar Press, 1976.

Chickering, Howell D., trans. *Beowulf: A Dual-Language Edition*. New York: Anchor Press/Doubleday, 1977.

Claiborne, Robert. *Our Marvelous Native Tongue: The Life and Times of the English Language*. New York: Times Books, 1983.

Clark, Cecily, ed. *The Peterborough Chronicle 1070-1154*, 2nd ed. London: Oxford University Press, 1970.

Clark, John W. *Early English: A Study of Old and Middle English*. London: André Deutsch, 1967.

Cockeram, Henry. *The English Dictionarie*, 1623. With a prefatory note by Chauncey Tinker. New York: Huntington Press, 1980.

Collins, Marie. *Caxton: The Description of Britain*. New York: Weidenfeld & Nicolson, 1988.

Diringer, David. *A History of the Alphabet*. London: Staples Press, 1977.

Elliott, Ralph W. V. *Runes: An Introduction*. Manchester, England: Manchester University Press, 1963.

Ford, Worthington C. *The Writings of George Washington. Vol. I: 1748-1757*. New York: G. P. Putnam, 1889.

Guralnik, David B. "Early English Dictionaries," 1951. In Charlton Laird and Robert M. Gorrell, eds., *English as Language: Backgrounds, Development, Usage*, 123-26. New York: Harcourt, Brace & World, 1961.

Hinman, Charlton, ed. *The First Folio of Shakespeare: The Norton Facsimile*. New York: W. W. Norton, 1968.

Hook, Julius N., and E.G. Mathews. *Modern American Grammar and Usage*. New York: Ronald Press, 1956.

Johnson, Samuel. 1755. *A Dictionary of the English Language.* 2 vols. London: Printed by W. Strahan for J. & P. Knapton, *et al.* Facsimile printed by AMS Press, New York, 1967.

Landau, Sidney. "Webster and Worcester: The War of the Dictionaries." *Wilson Library Bulletin*, 58 (April) 1984: 545-49.

Lowth, Robert. *A Short Introduction to English Grammar*, 1775. A facsimile reproduction with an introduction by Charlotte Downey. Delmar, NY: Scholars' Facsimiles & Reprints, 1979.

McCrum, Robert, William Cran, and Robert MacNeil. *The Story of English*. New York: Viking Penguin, 1986.

Miller, C. William. *Benjamin Franklin's Philadelphia Printing*. Philadelphia: American Philosophical Society, 1974.

Millward, Celia M. *A Biography of the English Language*. New York: Holt, Rinehart & Winston, 1989.

Monaghan, E. Jennifer. *A Common Heritage: Noah Webster's Blue-Back Speller*. Hamden, CT: Archon Books, 1983.

Mossé, Fernand. *A Handbook of Middle English*. Translated by James A. Walker. Baltimore: Johns Hopkins Press, 1952.

Myers, L. M. *The Roots of Modern English*. Boston: Little, Brown, 1966.

Nist, John. *A Structural History of English*. New York: St. Martin's Press, 1966.

Page, R. I. *Runes*. Berkeley: University of California Press, 1987.

Pope, Mildred K. *From Latin to Modern French with Especial Consideration of Anglo-Norman*. Manchester: Manchester University Press, 1934.

Pyles, Thomas, and John Algeo. *The Origins and Development of the English Language,* 3rd ed. New York: Harcourt Brace Jovanovich, 1982.

Roper, Alan, ed. *The Works of John Dryden,* vol. XIII. Berkeley: University of California Press, 1984.

Ruggiers, Paul G., ed. *The Canterbury Tales: A Facsimile and Transcription of the Hengwrt Manuscript, with Variants from the Ellesmere Manuscript*. Norman, OK: University of Oklahoma Press, 1979.

Savage, Anne, trans. *The Anglo-Saxon Chronicles*. New York: St. Martin's/Marek, 1983.

Spevack, Marvin. "Shakespeare's Language." In John F. Andrews, ed. *William Shakespeare: His World, His Work, His Influence,* vol. II, 343-95. New York: Charles Scribner's Sons, 1985.

Spisak, James W., ed. *Caxton's Malory: A New Edition of Sir Thomas Malory's Le Morte Darthur based on the Pierpont Morgan Copy of William Caxton's Edition of 1485*. Berkeley: University of California Press, 1983.

Webster, Noah. *Dissertations on the English Language*, 1789. Facsimile printed by The Scolar Press Limited, Menston, England, 1967.

__________. *A Compendious Dictionary of the English Language*. Hartford, CT: Hudson & Goodwin, 1806.

__________. *An American Dictionary of the English Language*, 2 vols., 1828. Facsimile printed by Johnson Reprint Corp., New York and London, 1970.

__________. *The American Spelling Book, Containing the Rudiments of the English Language for the Use of Schools in the United States*. Facsimile of the edition published in 1831 by William H. Niles, Middletown, CT. New York: Bureau of Publications, Teachers College, Columbia University, 1962.

Whitelock, Dorothy, ed. *The Peterborough Chronicle*. Copenhagen: Rosenkilde & Bagger, 1954

__________, ed. *The Anglo-Saxon Chronicle*. New Brunswick, NJ: Rutgers University Press, 1961.

Wright, David. *Geoffrey Chaucer: The Canterbury Tales. A Verse Translation*. Oxford and New York: Oxford University Press, 1985.

Yule, George. *The Study of Language: An Introduction*. Cambridge: Cambridge University Press, 1985.

Index